GIFTS F
Moses Maimonid

Translation and Introduction by Joseph B. Meszler

Second Edition, 2015

Reprinted with permission of:

Dr. Marc Lee Raphael, editor

Department of Religion
The College of William and Mary
Williamsburg, Virginia
2003

Table of Contents

Translator's Introduction

The problem of the destitute within society appears to be an eternal one. In fact, in Deuteronomy 15:11 we read, "There will never cease to be needy ones in your land."[1] One might read this as a pessimistic statement, an indication of a problem that will never be solved. The questions of what is the correct distribution of wealth, the best system by which to do so, and the most honorable care of the vulnerable members of society have not been challenges approaching resolution, even today with our increased technology and our ability to produce enough food to feed the entire world.

Nevertheless, in a different verse, we read the commandment not to "harden your heart and shut your hand against your needy kinsman. Rather, you must open your hand and lend him sufficient for whatever he needs" (Deuteronomy 15:7-8). Thus, scholars of the Jewish tradition have spent a great deal of energy thinking through the problem of taking care of the poor, both philosophically as well as through legal institutions, despite the enormity of the task. Jewish law demands that the Jewish community hope and strive for an ideal of seeing to the welfare of all people even if the ideal cannot be completely realized. We can still improve the lot of humankind.

That helping the poor was thought of as a matter of justice can be seen in the very name in Hebrew for charity, *tzedakah*, the root of which indicates "righteousness." Giving charity is not merely a matter of benevolence; it is the right thing to do in God's eyes. The English word "charity" is derived from the Latin "*caritas*," meaning, "love." *Tzedakah*, however, is mandated by law, regardless of one's sentiments. As one scholar has put it: "Jewish tradition, from the Bible onward, considers *tzedakah* to be a legal duty, a social responsibility, a repayment of a debt to God. Giving *tzedakah* is the fulfillment of a commandment rather than an act of optional benevolence."[2]

Today, many Jews find great spiritual satisfaction in the giving of *tzedakah*. It is a pillar of Jewish identity. For the Jew, there is more to the giving *tzedakah* than a mere transaction. There is a great spiritual depth and many ethical dimensions to the act. Consider, for instance, the names of the categories of agricultural produce that were designated for the poor. Certain agricultural produce, such as that which grew on the edge of the field, grain that was overlooked, grapes that were separated or malformed, and stalks that were

1. All biblical translations are taken from *Tanakh: The Holy Scriptures, the New JPS Translation According to the Traditional Hebrew Text* (Philadelphia: the Jewish Publication Society, 1988).
2. Byron L. Sherwin, *In Partnership With God*. (Syracuse: Syracuse University Press, 1990), 112.

forgotten, are listed in the Torah and designated by rabbis as belonging to the poor. These categories illustrate the rabbis' psychological astuteness, for in naming the categories of charity for the poor by these terms, they also described the types of people who commonly were destitute: the marginal, the overlooked, the forgotten, the separated, and the malformed or disabled. The association of the crop itself with the types of poor people serves as a reminder of their station, how easily they are dismissed and pushed to the "edges" of our consciousness and priorities, and of their need for our empathetic care.

In the giving of *tzedakah*, therefore, we can see from the earliest sources that more was intended than a material transaction. Empathy for the poor, sensitivity to who they are, their status in life, and the consciousness of the giver were all factors in the intention of the law.

Perhaps the most thoughtful treatise on the subject of *tzedakah* was written by Rabbi Moses Maimonides (1135-1204), known also by the honorific acronym of his name, Rambam. The title of his treatise is "Laws on Gifts for the Poor." It is important to note that the title of his treatise implies a theological statement. What is quickly apparent when reading this treatise is that the gifts of *tzedakah* are not only the gifts of the farmer or even the person who puts a coin in the charity coffer. Rather, these are assumed to be God's gifts to the poor, and human beings have the privilege of distributing wealth the way that God intended. Ultimately, it is assumed that "all wealth belongs to God," and it is up to the members of the community to distribute the wealth as God sees fit.[3] Beginning with agricultural, land-based produce and later evolving into monetary contributions, these sources of capital and sustenance are considered by Jewish tradition to belong to the poor from the start. Rather than an individual presuming ownership over some material good and then, as an act of benevolence, bestowing the food on a lowly person, the laws of *tzedakah* indicate that the poor own these gifts from God, and the giver is responsible for the stewardship of these material goods to their rightful owners.[4] These are God's gifts to the poor, and the members of the Jewish community have the privilege and responsibility of arranging the world the way that God intended so that the poor receive their due.

---

3. Solomon Schechter, "Jewish Philanthropy" in *Studies in Judaism, Third Series* (Philadelphia: The Jewish Publication Society of America, 1924), 241 as well as Elliott N. Dorff, *To Do The Right And The Good* (Philadelphia: Jewish Publication Society, 2002), 135.
4. Meir Tamari makes precisely this point when he writes, "By these laws, the belief in divine bounty as a source of all wealth creates in Judaism a concept of stewardship, whereby part of that wealth is given to assist others... If people really believed that all their needs would be satisfied as a result of God's mercy and providence, then they would not hesitate to share their wealth with others. Indeed, the refusal to share wealth with others is a denial of trust in God, a rejection of God's merit as the provider of the needs of man, and an assumption that that wealth is the result solely of one's work, ability, or luck." Meir Tamari, *The Challenge of Wealth* (Northvale, New Jersey: Jason Aronson Inc., 1995), 147-149.

The presumption here, very different from attitudes toward welfare in our own day, is that both the poor and the owner of property have God-given rights. The poor are entitled to the food that God has given them, and the owner of property has the right to designate and transfer these gifts. These assumptions provide an almost "constitutional" foundation for the laws of *tzedakah*.

Moses Maimonides and His Work

Maimonides transformed the way people thought about Jewish law. For some time before him, Jewish scholars tried to glean the correct way of practicing Judaism from the Jewish Bible (the *Tanakh*) and from a veritable encyclopedia of Jewish legend and legal debate, the Babylonian Talmud, as well as other sources. Maimonides set out to codify Jewish law in a systematic and all-encompassing approach in his work, the *Mishneh Torah*. The title of the work, written in Hebrew, indicates his audaciousness as well as his greatness, as it literally translates into "a Restatement of the Torah."

While the *Mishneh Torah* was met with great debate over its authority and its method, it has stood as one of the great legal works of Judaism. The *Mishneh Torah* shows the mind of a brilliant scholar who brought together hundreds of diverse and complex sources into a relatively easy-to-read manual that lists the *mitzvot*, the divine commandments, that Jews are to follow, regardless of whether or not they were directly applicable to Maimonides' contemporary scene. Jews, while in exile from the Land of Israel, without political sovereignty, and without the Temple in Jerusalem, could not practice many of the laws, but Maimonides was not chiefly concerned with immediate applicability. Maimonides sought to systematize the whole of Jewish law as it originated in the Torah until his day.

Maimonides is also remembered for another great book, the *Guide of the Perplexed*. In this work, written in Judeo-Arabic, Maimonides attempts to reconcile the rational philosophies of his day with the *Tanakh* and Jewish tradition. Well-schooled in the thoughts of Aristotle and Plato as presented by Muslim thinkers, Maimonides sought to explicate Jewish beliefs in light of these rational systems of thought and show there was no contradiction between them. It is invaluable to compare this philosophical work with the *Mishneh Torah*. Not only does the *Guide of the Perplexed* provide a philosophical background for the *Mishneh Torah*, it also serves as a basis for comparison with the *Mishneh Torah*'s more speculative sections as well as an explanation of Maimonides' theory of law. Every law, claims Maimonides, has a reason, and ultimately living in accordance with the law leads to the perfection of humanity.[5]

---

5. Moses Maimonides, *The Guide of the Perplexed*, translated by Shlomo Pines (Chicago: The University of Chicago Press, 1963), III:25-28, 502-514.

Sources for Maimonides' Treatise on Gifts for the Poor

We can see this operating principle, that the law is rational and leads to the perfection of humankind, at work in "Laws on Gifts for the Poor." In this section, found in the seventh volume of the *Mishneh Torah*, in the section called *Zeraim* or "Seeds," which focuses on agriculture, Maimonides systematized the laws of charity as they are presented in the *Tanakh* and other sources. Maimonides collected and organized different passages of law pertaining to how the Jewish Bible instructs the Israelites to gather agricultural produce and leave aside certain amounts for the poor and other vulnerable members of society. The most relevant passages of Scripture concerning agricultural produce in the Land of Israel include the following:

> When you reap the harvest of your land, you shall not reap all the way to the edges of your field, or gather the gleanings of your harvest. You shall not pick your vineyard bare, or gather the fallen fruit of your vineyard; you shall leave them for the poor and the stranger: I the Eternal am your God. (Leviticus 19:9-10)
>
> And when you reap the harvest of your land, you shall not reap all the way to the edges of the field, or gather the gleanings of your harvest; you shall leave them for the poor and the stranger: I the Eternal am your God. (Leviticus 23:22)
>
> Every third year you shall bring out the full tithe of your yield of that year, but leave it within your settlements. Then the Levite, who has no hereditary portion as you have, and the stranger, the fatherless, and the widow in your settlements shall come and eat their fill, so that the Eternal your God may bless you in all the enterprises you undertake. (Deuteronomy 14:28-29)
>
> When you reap the harvest in your field and overlook a sheaf in the field, do not turn back to get it; it shall go to the stranger, the fatherless, and the widow -- in order that the Eternal your God may bless you in all your undertakings. When you beat down the fruit of your olive trees, do not go over them again; that shall go to the stranger, the fatherless, and the widow. When you gather the grapes of your vineyard, do not pick it over again; that shall go to the stranger, the fatherless, and the widow. Always remember that you were a slave in Egypt; therefore do I enjoin you to observe this commandment. (Deuteronomy 24:19-22)

Maimonides looks to other parts of the Torah for non-agrarian methods of charity as well. Among these biblical sources, he refers to the following:

> If, however, there is a needy person among you, one of your kinsmen in any of your settlements in the land that the Eternal your God is giving you, do not harden your heart and shut your hand against your needy kinsman. Rather, you must open your hand and lend him sufficient for whatever he needs... For there will never cease to be needy ones in your land, which is why I command you: open your hand to the poor and needy kinsman in your land. (Deuteronomy 15:7-8, 11)

> If your kinsman, being in straits comes under your authority, and you hold him as though a resident alien, let him live by your side: do not exact from him advance or accrued interest, but fear your God. Let him live by your side as your kinsman. (Leviticus 25:35-36)

In addition to these sources as well as other passages in the *Tanakh*, Maimonides also relied upon other sources of Jewish law. It has been pointed out that in his introduction to the *Mishneh Torah* as well as in a letter to a fellow scholar, Maimonides claims his sources include the *Mishnah*, the *Tosefta*, the Babylonian and Jerusalem Talmuds, and the commentaries *Sifra* and *Sifre*.[6] The *Mishnah* is a compilation of Jewish law redacted by the year 200 C.E., and the *Tosefta* is additional material of roughly the same time period as the *Mishnah* but not included in it. The main focus of relevant law in these sources was the tractate entitled, *Péah*, after the Hebrew word for the "edge" of the field mentioned in Leviticus 19:9 and 23:22. This tractate contains some of the earliest legislation based upon these biblical passages. For later material, Maimonides referred to the Babylonian Talmud for sources on charity, which serves as an elaboration and extension of most of the teachings found in the *Mishnah*.

However, it is interesting to note that the Babylonian Talmud does not contain commentary upon tractate *Péah*, the most relevant source of rabbinic law. However, commentary on tractate *Péah* may be found in the Jerusalem Talmud, a work produced in the Land of Israel of smaller and earlier scope than the Babylonian Talmud. Maimonides does not draw heavily from the Jerusalem Talmud in this treatise, nor does he explicitly cite much material from *Sifra* and

---

6. Abraham Cronbach, "The Maimonidean Code of Benevolence" in *Hebrew Union College Annual XX 1947* (New York: Ktav Publishing House, Inc., 1968), 471.

Sifre, collections of rabbinic interpretation on Leviticus, Numbers, and Deuteronomy.

It is chiefly for not citing the Jerusalem Talmud frequently that the scholar Rabbi Abraham ben David of Posquiéres (c.1120-1197) interjects some criticisms into the "Laws on Gifts for the Poor." Rabbi Abraham ben David, most commonly known by the acronym of his name, Ravad, was one of Maimonides' chief critics, and his commentary is customarily published alongside Maimonides' elucidation of the law in the *Mishneh Torah*.[7] With regard to this specific treatise, however, Ravad's criticisms are relatively few in number, but summaries of his comments are provided in the annotations to the following translation to provide a legal counterpoint to Maimonides' rulings.

A source of frustration in studying the treatise, as well as a challenge against the authority of the *Mishneh Torah* as a source of Jewish law, is that Maimonides did not explicitly cite his sources. While we know the volumes that he consulted for his decision-making, we do not know the precise passages. Sometimes Maimonides is clearly quoting another earlier, authoritative work, while at other times he is using his own reason. It is for this reason that a reader of the *Mishneh Torah* must, in the words of Abraham Cronbach, take an "elastic" approach to how Maimonides makes reference to earlier works of Jewish law.[8] Even when Maimonides makes implicit reference to a well-known passage from the Babylonian Talmud or other work, he often does so with interpretation. Rarely does he cite something word for word. In addition, there are times when he clearly makes reference to a text that he did not list in his introduction. For instance, near the end of the treatise in 10:5, Maimonides quotes from Leviticus Rabbah 34:15, a collection of rabbinic interpretation that he did not mention as one of his sources, claiming that if one does not have something to give a beggar, one should at least speak to the poor person kindly. This gap could have come about for a variety of reasons, including that Maimonides could have simply failed to list an important work of Jewish teaching.

In the annotations of the following translation, one is invited to look at relevant sources and compare them to Maimonides' writing, but there is rarely an exact correspondence. For the faithful Jew who is trying to figure out which is the correct practice to follow, the lack of explicit citations makes Maimonides' decisions suspect. For the student of history and philosophy, however, this

---

7. See Isadore Twersky, *Rabad of Posquiéres: A Twelfth-Century Talmudist* (Cambridge: Harvard University Press, 1962).
8. Cronbach, 475. Cronbach also studied the work of scholars who in the past have tried to find all of Maimonides' sources, including Joseph Caro (1488-1575) in the *Kesef Mishnah*, David ben Solomon ibn Abi Zimra (1479-1589), the citations of the Venice edition published by Giustiniani in 1550, and Joshua Boas in *Ein Mishpat* of the 16th century, and he found all of them lacking.

presents an opportunity to discover how Maimonides thought, especially when held in comparison with the *Guide of the Perplexed.*

It is precisely in comparison with the sources that Maimonides chose to cite as well as the passages that Maimonides chose to leave behind that we see his rationale and philosophy of Jewish law. Specifically, in comparing "Laws on Gifts for the Poor" to the *Guide of the Perplexed* as well as sources of Jewish law, we see that, for Maimonides, the practice of *tzedakah* was not only a method of bettering society but also a path of virtue.

The Structure of the Treatise

Before we make this comparison, let us first understand the form and content of Maimonides' treatise on charity. If we examine the structure of "Laws on Gifts for the Poor," we see that Maimonides wrote ten chapters on the subject. An outline of the treatise is as follows:

Chapter 1 -- An overview of the biblical laws of agricultural gifts for the poor: *péah* - the "edge" of standing crops, *leket* - "overlooked gleanings," *peret* - "separated fruit," *olélot* - "malformed grape clusters," and *shikhecha* - the "forgotten."
Chapters 2 & 3 – *Péah.*
Chapter 4:1-14 – *Leket.*
Chapter 4:15-16 – *Peret.*
Chapter 4:17-27 – *Olélot.*
Chapter 5:1-26 – *Shikhecha.*
Chapter 5:27 -- Concluding remark about all five categories in relation to *hefker* ("ownerless property").
Chapter 6 -- *Ma'esar Ani* ("the tithe for the poor").
Chapter 7 -- General laws of *tzedakah*: how much, from whom, and to whom.
Chapter 8:1-5 -- Pledges to *tzedakah* and laws of vows.
Chapter 8:6-9 -- Donations to the Jewish community and relations to the Gentile community.
Chapter 8:10-18 -- The redemption of captives.
Chapter 9:1-7 -- Contemporary institutions: the "charity coffer" and the "charity plate."
Chapter 9:8-19 -- Rules for collectors of *tzedakah.*
Chapter 10:1-6 -- Motivation to give and collect *tzedakah.*
Chapter 10:7-14 -- Eight levels of giving.
Chapter 10:15-19 -- Examples of the ideal ways of giving *tzedakah.*

Maimonides claims that there are thirteen commandments from the Torah that apply to *tzedakah.* The first ten are five pairs derived from the previously cited biblical passages. The pairs consist of an injunction to leave behind certain agricultural produce for the poor and a complementary prohibition against the impulse to gather the produce. The categories of agricultural produce designated for the poor derived from the Torah total five: *péah* - the "edge" of the field, *leket* - "overlooked gleanings" that the farmer missed as he went through the field, *peret* - "separated fruit" of a vineyard consisting of a stem with one or two grapes, *olélot* - "malformed grape clusters" that one could not sell at market value, and *shikhecha* - the "forgotten" produce that the farmer left behind and remembered later. The categories of *peret* and *olélot* apply only to the vineyard while the category of *leket* applies only to the field. *Péah* and *shikhecha* apply to every situation. Maimonides, in the first five chapters of "Laws on Gifts for the Poor," addresses these five categories, defining these terms legally and illustrating their practice as it would take place in the Land of Israel under Jewish law.

Some of the other questions Maimonides addresses, based upon traditional sources, in these first five chapters are: How much does the Israelite farmer need to leave? What qualifies as *péah, leket,* etc.? How do partners who own a field jointly follow the laws of charity? When and how is the produce distributed? How are certain kinds of produce, such as onions or olives, which do not fall neatly into the general categories of a field of grain or a vineyard, treated with regard to these laws? How do relations with non-Jewish neighbors affect these practices?[9]

In the sixth chapter, Maimonides deals with the tithe for the poor, *ma'esar ani,* as mentioned in Deuteronomy 14:28-29. In a seven-year cycle of tithes, the Torah instructs that in the third year a tithe be taken that is designated for "the Levite, who has no hereditary portion as you have, and the stranger, the fatherless, and the widow." The stranger, the fatherless, and the widow, that is, the vulnerable members of society, came to represent the destitute. In this chapter, Maimonides illustrates the system of tithes and the distribution of the tithe for the poor.

In chapters seven, eight, and nine, however, Maimonides changes the focus of the treatise. Rather than focus upon the agrarian methods of charity as described

---

9. Several times in the treatise, it is noted that one gives produce to the poor of Gentiles "for the sake of peaceful relations." (See 1:9, for example.) Elliot Dorff reminds us to "remember that until the twentieth century most Jewish lived in societies that were corporately organized, in which each ethnic or religious group within a nation had responsibility for dealing with its own internal affairs. Moreover, under Muslims and Christians, Jews were generally second-class citizens who had as little contact with non-Jews as possible. That Jewish law should require Jews to give charity to non-Jews at all – even if it is only for the political motive for maintaining peace – is, therefore, remarkable." Dorff, 143.

in the Torah, Maimonides turns to later legal institutions that had direct relevance to his contemporary scene. Maimonides introduces institutions of charity that are mentioned in the Babylonian Talmud that apply to urban as well as agrarian situations. The three methods of distributing charity that Maimonides elucidates are begging, the charity coffer (*kupah*), which is a general fund that is distributed weekly to the poor, and the charity plate (*tamchui*), which is distributed daily. Some understand the *tamchui* to be the equivalent of today's soup kitchen, that is, a daily distribution of food.[10]

With regards to begging, Maimonides describes the way and the amount one should give to beggars, including the principle found in the Babylonian Talmud (such as in Ketubot 67b) that one should fill a needy person's lack, taking into account the dignity of his or her background. He explains that one is not obligated to make someone wealthy again, but he does imply that one who has fallen from a high station has special psychological needs.

Maimonides also describes in one passage the relevance of family and community ties to giving to the poor, explaining that closest family takes first priority, then extended relatives, then the members of one's town, and so on.[11]

It should be noted that, in the biblical commandments regarding *tzedakah*, the individual is addressed. In the agrarian methods of setting aside grain and other produce for the poor, the individual Israelite is the central figure. In the chapters concerning the *kupah* and the *tamchui*, however, Maimonides turns the focus to the community as a whole. Maimonides describes public assistance to the poor as invented by the rabbis of antiquity and speaks of the obligations of the Jewish people as a group. As Isadore Twersky writes, "*Tzedakah* thus emerges as an individual obligation which is fulfilled corporately."[12]

---

10. Frank M. Loewenberg, *From Charity to Social Justice: The Emergence of Communal Institutions for the Support of the Poor in Ancient Judaism* (New Brunswick: Transaction Publishers, 2001), 120-122.
11. One might think that one need only take care of one's own family and otherwise not give. Subsequent thinking of Jewish legal scholars have held that this is not what Maimonides intended. See Aaron Levine, *Economics & Jewish Law* (Hoboken: KTAV Publishing House, Inc, 1987, 117-118) where he summarizes some of the interpretations of this passage and points out that Rabbi Pinchas Halevi Horowitz (Germany, ca. 1731-1805, quoted in R. Moses Sofer, Hungary, 1762-1839, *Chatam Sofer, Yoreh De'ah*, 144) understands this hierarchy in prioritizing giving to be qualified by the urgency of need. A life-threatening emergency to a stranger overrides gifts to one's family. Rabbi Yechiel Michel Epstein (Belorussia, 1829-1908, as cited in Levine, *Aruch Hashulchan*, op. cit. 251:4) understands Maimonides' statement to indicate priorities in the amount given but not that one excludes a needy person. Finally, Rabbi Mosheh Feinstein (New York, 1895-1986, as cited in Levine, *Iggerot Mosheh, Yoreh De'ah*, 144) claims that relative need is only applicable to public funds, but the private distribution of charity can be given in whatever manner the donor chooses.
12. Isadore Twersky, *Studies in Jewish Law and Philosophy* (New York: KTAV Publishing House, Inc., 1982), 117. See also Loewenberg, 120, where he writes, "It became more and

Maimonides also describes the duties of those who collect and distribute charity, both through the *kupah* and the *tamchui*. He sees their role as one of a trustee that makes determinations of fact. They decide what is best in any given situation of financial need and operate open to public scrutiny. At the same time, collectors of *tzedakah* must act confidentially in order to protect the dignity of those who receive *tzedakah*. He also makes explicit that, first and foremost, collectors and distributors of *tzedakah* need to be honest and competent. Maimonides brings in relevant tangential subjects such as that a pledge to *tzedakah* is the equivalent of a legal vow and that other needs, including donations to a synagogue or the redemption of captives, must be considered and prioritized. This last subject, the redemption of captives, is meditated on at great length because of the seriousness of the threat to life by hostile ruling powers. A member or leader of the Jewish community could be held for ransom, and it was up to the generosity and the financial resources of the community to pay for their leader's safe return. The laws regarding the redemption of captives indicate the precarious position in which the Jewish community occasionally found itself. It is telling that Maimonides only prescribes giving to the poor of Gentiles along with those of the Jewish community if this is "for the sake of peace," that is, for sake of political expediency.

The Final Chapter: A Sermon

Finally, in Chapter Ten, Maimonides describes the ethics of giving charity, so that the final chapter reads more like a sermon than a code of law. Within the chapter, he gives four philosophical rationales for why Jews should give charity.

The first reason that stands out in Maimonides' treatise on the poor is the integrity of one's lineage. Maimonides clearly states that giving *tzedakah* is a basic characteristic of the Jewish people, inherited directly from Abraham. Without this aspect of generosity and compassion, one's lineage becomes suspect. In Maimonides own words, we read:

> We must be especially careful to observe the *mitzvah* of *tzedakah*, more so than any other positive *mitzvah*, for *tzedakah* is a sign of the righteous [*tzadik*] lineage of Abraham, our father, as it

more difficult for the biblical charity system to cope with the grown needs of the poor, a population whose numbers expanded markedly during the latter centuries of the Second Temple period. The charitable institutions that were based on individual initiative were no longer adequate... The communal poor relief scheme of urban sectarians...may have been the first example of a communal institution for the poor in ancient Judea... In time it became evident that the new societal conditions made it imperative to supplement individual efforts for the poor with communal institutions."

> is said, (Genesis 18:19) *For I have singled him out, that he may instruct his children and his posterity [to keep the way of the Eternal] by doing what is just [tzedakah] and right...* And if someone is cruel and without compassion, then his lineage is suspect, for cruelty is only found among the idolatrous nations, as it is said, (Jer. 50:42) *They are cruel, they show no mercy.* (10:1-2)

Charity, then, is basic to the essence of the people of Israel. Maimonides preaches that one cannot be Jewish without being charitable; Jewish identity and generosity are interdependent. It is for this reason that Maimonides also claims that

> the throne of Israel is established and the religion of truth stands only on *tzedakah*, as it is said, (Isaiah 54:14) *You shall be established through righteousness [tzedek].* (10:1)

In other words, Israel's existence and authenticity depend upon their practice of charity. The act of charity and the value of righteousness are one and the same and form the basis for the religion. Not only that, but the integrity of the nation rests upon the charitableness of its citizens, or else Judaism will not be a "religion of truth."

So important and basic is *tzedakah* to the Jewish people that Maimonides also claims that there will be no redemption without the practice of charity. In the first law in Chapter 10 he states:

> And Israel will only be redeemed through *tzedakah*, as it is said, (Isaiah 1:27) *Zion shall be saved in the judgment; her repentant ones, in justice [tzedakah].*[13]

Without the practice of charity, Maimonides teaches, the Jewish connection to the past is suspect, its claims of truth in the present are falsified, and its future redemption is put in doubt. Maimonides thus begins the rationale for Jewish people to give *tzedakah* by claiming that it is so basic to Jewish tradition that without it, all else is lost.

After this lofty language, Maimonides then gives a second reason for giving charity that is more practical, and one might say desperate, in nature. This reason is kinship. Very simply put, the Jewish community needed to be self-sufficient because there was no one else to take care of the vulnerable members of the

---

13. The JPS translation here reads "retribution" instead of "justice," but that would make the homiletical device confusing.

Jewish community other than the Jews themselves. A tie of kinship, therefore, was a connection of responsibility. As Maimonides says,

> All Israel and all who are associated with them are like brothers, as it is said, (Deut. 14:1) *You are children of the Eternal your God.* And if a brother does not show compassion for another brother, then who will have compassion for him? And to whom can the poor of Israel look? To the idolatrous nations that hate them and pursue them? They can only look to rely upon their brothers.

In a very practical and immediate sense of need, then, without the value of kinship, the Jewish poor were doomed. If a Jew did not feel responsibility for another Jew as for a family member and did not provide support to vulnerable members of the Jewish community, they would be left exposed to the hostile ruling powers that cared nothing about whether a Jewish person lived or died.

As was noted earlier, the responsibility of kinship also applied within one's own family as well as outside of it. Maimonides writes, "one should give sustenance to one's father and mother, for this is essential *tzedakah*. It is an important principle of *tzedakah* that a relative takes precedence [over another]" (10:16). Immediate family needed to be taken care of first. As for those who had no immediate family, such as widows and orphans, Maimonides makes special mention of how important it is to still consider them as kin so they do not get left behind (10:17).

Essential to this obligation that came with kinship was also a bond of empathy and compassion. Maimonides has only the harshest words for those who neglect their Jewish "brothers," calling them "wicked" and "sinners" (10:3). He therefore explains that one should not only give *tzedakah* but one should do so in a sensitive way with kind words and a compassionate expression.

> Anyone who gives *tzedakah* to a poor person with a scowl and causes him to be embarrassed, even if he gave him a thousand *zuz*, has destroyed and lost any merit thereby. Rather, one should give cheerfully, with happiness [to do so] and empathy for his plight, as it is said, (Job 30:25) *Did I not weep for the unfortunate? Did I not grieve for the needy?* And one should speak to him words of comfort and consolation, as it is said, (Job 29:13) *[I received the blessing of the lost,] I gladdened the heart of the widow.* (10:4)

With this description of how to give *tzedakah* and interact with the needy comes a passionate plea for empathy on behalf of the poor. Maimonides not only tells his readers that, "it is forbidden to speak harshly to a poor person or to raise your voice in a shout, for his heart is broken and crushed," (10:5), but he also threatens that one provokes God's wrath by showing cruelty to the poor. Unkindness is paid back with unkindness. He writes:

> The Holy One, Blessed Be He, is close to the cries of the poor, as it is said, (Job 34:28) *He listens to the cry of the needy.* Therefore, one needs to be especially sensitive to their cries, for they [the poor] have a covenant established [between them and God], as it is said, (Exodus 22:26) *Therefore, if he cries out to Me, I will pay heed, for I am compassionate*... Thus it says in Scripture, (Psalms 51:19) *God, You will not despise a contrite and crushed heart.* And it says, (Isaiah 57:15) *Reviving the spirits of the lowly, reviving the hearts of the contrite.* And woe to anyone who shames a poor person! Woe to him! Rather, let him be like a father to him, in compassion and in words, as it is said, (Job 29:15) *I was a father to the needy.* (10:3-5)

In the bonds of kinship, therefore, Maimonides does not simply say that compassion would be a nice characteristic in giving charity. Rather, God is intimately involved in the giving of *tzedakah* and is sensitive to how it is done. While not saying so explicitly, Maimonides seems to be invoking the ethic, *Love your fellow as yourself* (Lev. 19:18) to describe how the responsibility toward kin should be.

There is also a third overriding philosophical rationale found in this chapter in addition to integrity as a nation and the loving bonds of kinship, namely, that the act of giving *tzedakah* is one of virtue that ennobles the giver. Maimonides implies this belief in the elevating power of philanthropy in one of his most famous writings, the eight degrees of charity, where he illustrates the highest versus the lowest forms of giving charity and the levels in between. Maimonides' eight levels of *tzedakah* are:

> There are eight levels of *tzedakah*, each one greater than the other. The greatest level, higher than all the rest, is to fortify a fellow Jew and give him a gift, a loan, form with him a partnership, or find work for him, until he is strong enough so that he does not need to ask others [for sustenance]... One level lower than this is one who gives *tzedakah* to the poor and does not know to whom he gives, and the poor person does not know from whom he receives... One level lower is one who gives *tzedakah* and the giver knows to whom he gives but the poor person does not know

> from whom he takes... One level lower is when the poor person knows from whom he takes but the giver does not know to whom he gives... One level lower is to give to him with one's own hand before he can ask. One level lower is to give to him after he has asked. One level lower is to give him less than one should but with kindness. One level lower is to give to him begrudgingly. (10:7-14)[14]

One explanation of these levels is that Maimonides and other Jewish scholars understood that "just as there were levels and degrees of aid, so were there levels and degrees of need. It is noteworthy, and perhaps not coincidental, that Maimonides identified eight levels of *tzedakah*, while a rabbinic interpretation notes that biblical Hebrew has eight words to denote the poor."[15] Maimonides' hierarchy of *tzedakah* may have been a method of harmonizing opposing viewpoints in rabbinic literature. "Rather than present opposing views as contradictions, Maimonides placed these diffuse and often conflicting opinions as points on a spectrum. On one side is the altruistic donor who preserves the individuality and dignity of the person in need. On the other side is the self-serving or reluctant donor who must be cajoled into giving."[16]

We can see from this hierarchy that eliminating the need for charity by enabling a needy person to recover economic independence takes highest precedence. After this, when one is already in a situation in which charity needs to be given, giving anonymously, without the giver or the receiver knowing one

---

14. An obvious question is why does Maimonides claim that there are eight levels of giving and not some other number. While it would be premature to come to a definite conclusion, for the number could reflect personal inspiration, another possibility suggests itself from the Muslim world in which Maimonides lived. As reflected in the Islamic code of law, *The Reliance of the Traveller* by Ahmad ibn Naqib al-Misri (1301 – 1368), who lived in Cairo a century after Maimonides lived but who codified law that was in existence during Maimonides' time, we see that there are eight groups of people who are worthy to receive "*zakat*," that is, charity incumbent upon Muslims and one of the five pillars of Islam. See Ahmad ibn Naqib al-Misri, *Reliance of the Traveller*, translated by Nu Ha Mim Keller (Beltsville, Maryland: Amana Publications, 1994). The poor are divided according to Muslim law into eight categories of recipients who qualify to benefit from charity collected by the Muslim community. While the only connection between the two codes of law appears to be the number eight and the subject of charity, it is entirely possible that Maimonides, well aware of the basic practices of the Muslim world around him, may have found his inspiration from the Muslim community. Maimonides' relationship to the Muslim community and its impact on his writing is well-known in terms of his philosophy but still needs to be investigated in terms of his theory of law.
15. Sherwin, 107, on *Vayikra Rabbah* 34:6. In English, see Leviticus Rabbah (London: The Soncino Press, 1983).
16. Sherwin, 118.

another, is the best method for giving charity, as is ideally accomplished with the institution of the *kupah*, the "charity coffer," a weekly collection where donations were put into a box and then distributed by a competent authority to the poor. If the anonymity of one party needs to be sacrificed, Maimonides would have the giver remain anonymous so that the poor would not know the giver's identity and feel embarrassment in the giver's presence and the virtue of the giver would be upheld. However, this would also indicate that the poverty of the recipient has become known. The lower levels uphold the virtues of generosity and compassion, but we can also note that even giving charity begrudgingly still counts as a form of *tzedakah*.

A final word must also be mentioned about the value that Maimonides holds for the dignity of each human being. Just as the practice of *tzedakah* ennobles the giver, so must the honor of the receiver be upheld. An expression Maimonides frequently uses is that the poor may not become embarrassed, but the Hebrew literally means that one's face should not fall. In this spirit, Rabbi Solomon Schechter quotes the Babylonian Talmud Berachot 6b when he writes, "The degradation of the poor is pictured in various ways. 'When a person has to take charity, his face changes color, in a manner similar to that of the *Kerum*' – a certain bird which was supposed to have been found near the sea, and which, in sunshine, assumed various colors."[17] The face of the poor would literally blanche at the humiliation one might feel in taking *tzedakah* publicly.

Even in the cases of agricultural gifts for the poor as stated in the Torah, there is concern for the dignity of the poor, and this is emphasized by Maimonides throughout his treatise. The law states explicitly in Leviticus 19 that the poor should come and harvest the crop themselves rather than receive a handout. The prohibitions against harvesting all of one's field, gleaning all of one's crop, or gathering all that one might have forgotten (1:2, 4-5) do not just serve to inculcate self-restraint in the citizen; they also allow the poor the dignity of self-sufficiency.

Being self-sufficient, however, also must be complemented by being humble. Dignity is different than pride. Maimonides writes:

> One should always strain oneself and endure hardship and not come to depend on others rather than cast oneself onto the community. Thus the sages commanded, "Make your Sabbaths into weekdays rather than come to depend on others." Even if one is wise and revered and becomes poor, he should engage in some kind of craft, even a menial one, rather than come to depend on others. Better to stretch leather from carrion than to say, "I am a

17. Schecter, 261.

great sage," [or] "I am a priest. Feed me." Thus the sages commanded. Great sages were splitters of wood, raisers of beams, drawers of water for gardens, iron workers, and blacksmiths rather than ask [for their living] from the community or accept anything when they gave to them. (10:18)

In this spirit, it is no wonder that the highest level of giving *tzedakah* is giving a loan or a job so as to prevent poverty before it happens and to protect someone from slipping downwards. Working for one's living is better than living off *tzedakah.*

Maimonides makes other references to the idea that the poor must be protected from humiliation, either by giving them work or by giving to them in secret. He deals directly with this scenario in the case of a poor person who could be asked to give *tzedakah* but has nothing to give and would be embarrassed in public if he was asked in front of others.

> If a man who is of a generous mind gives *tzedakah* more than he should, or who afflicts himself and gives to the collectors so as not to be embarrassed, it is forbidden to make a claim of him or collect *tzedakah* from him. The collector who shames him or asks [for *tzedakah*] from him in the future will be punished, as it is said, (Jeremiah 30:20) *I will deal with all his oppressors.* (7:11)

The idea that the dignity of the poor must be protected is taken to an extreme in Jewish sources. Apparently based on the actions of Hillel in the Babylonian Talmud, Ketubot 67b, Maimonides claims:

> One is commanded to give to a poor person according to what he lacks... Even if it was the custom of [a person who was rich but is now] a poor person to ride on a horse with a servant running in front of him, and this is a person who fell from his station, they buy him a horse to ride upon and a servant to run in front of him, as it is said, (Deut. 15:8) *Sufficient for whatever he needs.* (7:3)

The dignity of each person is so important that one should go to the extreme of treating royalty like royalty even when they no longer have the wealth of their status. This principle, derived directly from the Torah, is psychologically insightful to the fact that different people have different experiences, expectations, and needs and therefore require special treatment. Included in the values of integrity, kinship, and virtue is a belief in the respect due to each person made in the image of God.

Maimonides and Rabbinic Literature

Maimonides' work on *tzedakah* did not occur in a vacuum. As was noted, much of his treatise is a compilation of existing rabbinic laws. The philosophy behind many of these laws also derives from rabbinic sources. For instance, the high priority Maimonides gives to the practice of *tzedakah* can be found in numerous sources, such as how God considers the poor to be close to Him. One source says, "When Israel asked God: 'Who are Thy people?' The reply was: 'The poor,' for it says, (Isaiah 49:13) *For the Eternal has comforted His people, and has taken back His afflicted ones [the poor] in love.*[18] As God's close associates, treating them justly and kindly is of utmost importance. Another rabbinic saying has it that God accompanies the poor as they beg, and to stand in front of a poor person is to stand before God.[19]

In addition, we find precedents for Maimonides' prescription that all Israel are duty-bound to each other as brothers in a remarkable story that contrasts how the rabbis perceived their pagan neighbors' practices with their own practice of charity.

> This question was actually put by Turnus Rufus to Rabbi Akiva: 'If your God loves the poor, why does He not support them?'
>
> He replied, 'So that we may be saved through them from the punishment of Gehinnom.'
>
> 'On the contrary,' said the other, 'it is this which condemns you to Gehinnom. I will illustrate by a parable. Suppose an earthly king was angry with his servant and put him in prison and ordered that he should be given no food or drink, and a man went and gave him food and drink. If the king heard, would he not be angry with him? And you are called "servants," as it is written, (Leviticus 25:55) *For it is to Me that the Israelites are servants.*
>
> Rabbi Akiva answered him: 'I will illustrate by another parable. Suppose an earthly king was angry with his son, and put him in prison and ordered that no food or drink should be given to him, and someone went and gave him food and drink. If the king heard of it, would he not send him a present? And we are called

18. *Shemot Rabbah* 31:5; translation taken from Exodus Rabbah (London: The Soncino Press, 1983). The language of other translations, whether lofty ("thee" and "thy") or in the vernacular has been preserved, but transliterations have been altered for the sake of consistency.
19. *Vayikra Rabbah* 34:9.

"children," as it is written, (Deuteronomy 14:1) *You are children of the Eternal your God.'*[20]

In this parable, the critical change between the Roman's point of view and Rabbi Akiva's is in viewing the people Israel as children of God. The parable implies that, while some might claim that poverty is a divine punishment, it is not the place of human beings to judge another because they are poor but rather to obey the commandment to help them. If all Israel are children of God, that makes each member of Israel a sibling, united in kinship. This idea can also be found in the Torah itself, in that the poor person is called "brother."[21] This is but one example; Maimonides writes from a large tradition of Israel regarding themselves as kin and responsible for one another.

As for the idea that the highest level of charity takes the form of a gift or a loan, even to the point where it is permissible to deceive someone too full of pride to accept *tzedakah*, we find this point of view in the case of Rabbi Yonah.

> Rabbi Yonah, when he saw a person of a respectable family who had lost his money and was ashamed to take charity, used to go to him and say to him: 'As I have heard that you have come into an inheritance somewhere abroad, I offer you this article, and when you are in better circumstances you will give it me back.' At the same time when he gave it to him he would say to him: 'I have given it to you as a gift.'[22]

As for the lowest end of the eight levels of charity, we may understand why Maimonides chose to put giving charity begrudgingly or with harsh words at the bottom. A general rabbinic principle regarding *tzedakah* is "the reward of charity depends entirely upon the extent of the kindness in it."[23] Without kindness, the deed loses merit.

However, we learn just as much about Maimonides' philosophy of *tzedakah* from what he includes as what he leaves out. Maimonides clearly rejects some notions in rabbinic thought. For instance, a very common belief found in the Babylonian Talmud and elsewhere that Maimonides does not cite any where in this legislation is that *tzedakah* has a magical effect of protecting one's life. In Proverbs 10:2 we read, *Tzedakah (charity/righteousness) saves from death.* Many

---

20. Babylonian Talmud, Bava Batra 10a. All translations are taken from *The Soncino Talmud* (Brooklyn, NY: Judaica Press, Inc., 1973 and Soncino Press, Ltd., 1965, 1967, 1977, 1983, 1984, 1987, 1988, 1990).
21. Leviticus 25:25, etc.
22. *Vayikra Rabbah* 34:1.
23. Babylonian Talmud Sukkah 49b, as explained in Twersky, 120.

passages in the Babylonian Talmud explore this adage through the use of parables. It is such a popular notion that it is included in the liturgy of the High Holy Days, where *tzedakah* is counted among those things that "avert God's decree."[24] Maimonides, however, deliberately leaves this proverb and its parables out of his treatise.

One can understand why Maimonides left out these references when one looks at the parables themselves. One of the places where we see the Talmud explore this commonly cited proverb about charity is in the context of a debate about astrology. Some rabbis argued that the planets decree the destiny of individuals, while others claimed that the planets have no control over the people of Israel. Rather, it is the practice of *mitzvot* that determine a Jew's destiny. Thus we have the following story:

> From Shemuel too [we learn that] Israel is immune from planetary influence. For Shemuel and Avlat were sitting, while certain people were going to a lake. Said Avlat to Shemuel: 'That man is going but will not return, [for] a snake will bite him and he will die.'
>
> 'If he is an Israelite,' replied Shemuel, 'he will go and return.'
>
> While they were sitting he went and returned. [Thereupon] Avlat arose and threw off his [the man's] knapsack, [and] found a snake therein cut up and lying in two pieces — Said Shemuel to him, 'What did you do?'
>
> 'Every day we pooled our bread and ate it; but to-day one of us had no bread, and he was ashamed. Said I to them, "I will go and collect [the bread]". When I came to him, I pretended to take [bread] from him, so that he should not be ashamed.'
>
> 'You have done a good deed,' said he to him. Then Shemuel went out and lectured (Proverbs 10:2): Tzedakah *saves from death.* And [this does not mean] from an unnatural death, but from death itself.[25]

Here, we read a story about how, according to astrological projections, a man's time to die had come, yet the practice of *tzedakah* saved him from death's decree, extending his life beyond what he would have normally been destined to live. The Talmudic debate here centers around whether the planets control one's destiny or something else. This passage of the Talmud implies that it is the practice of *mitzvot*, specifically *tzedakah*, which impacts a Jew's fate due to the

---

24. In the prayer, *Unataneh Tokef*, found in the High Holy Day prayer book.
25. Babylonian Talmud, Shabbat 156b.

providence of God, and not any other power. A passage with a similar philosophy pertaining to this proverb comes from another part of the Babylonian Talmud:

> It has been taught: Rabbi Yehudah says: Great is charity, in that it brings the redemption nearer, as it says (Isaiah 56:1), thus said the Eternal: Observe what is right and do what is just [*tzedakah*]; for soon My salvation shall come, and my deliverance shall be revealed.
>
> He also used to say: Ten strong things have been created in the world. The rock is hard, but the iron cleaves it. The iron is hard, but the fire softens it. The fire is hard, but the water quenches it. The water is strong, but the clouds bear it. The clouds are strong, but the wind scatters them. The wind is strong, but the body bears it. The body is strong, but fright crushes it. Fright is strong, but wine banishes it. Wine is strong, but sleep works it off. Death [which is the ultimate in sleep] is stronger than all, and charity saves from death, as it is written (Proverbs 10:2), Tzedakah *saves from death.*[26]

In this passage, Rabbi Yehudah preaches the rewards of *tzedakah* based upon a quotation from the prophet Isaiah. He then goes into a long chain of elemental forces in a person's life, the penultimate of which is death. However, even death is trumped by the act of *tzedakah*, which, it was believed, prolonged the giver's life in divinely ordained ways.

While stories and passages such as this one are numerous,[27] one more story from another source in a colorful translation by Judah Goldin will further illustrate the popularity of this belief.

> There was once a saint who was habitually charitable. One time he set out in a boat; a wind rose and sank his boat in the sea. Rabbi Akiva witnessed this and came before the court to testify that his wife might remarry. Before he could take the stand, the man came back and stood before him.
>
> "Art thou not he who went down in the sea?" Rabbi Akiva said to him.
>
> "Yes," he replied.
>
> "And who raised thee up out of the sea?"

26. Babylonian Talmud, Bava Batra 10a.
27. See also other stories and passages in the Babylonian Talmud Bava Batra 10a-b as well as Rosh Hashanah 16b, for example.

"The charity which I practiced," he answered; "it raised me out of the sea."

"How dost thou know this?" Rabbi Akiva inquired.

He said to him: "When I sank to the depths of the sea, I heard the sound of a great noise of the waves of the sea, one wave saying to the other and the other to another 'Hurry! And let us raise this man out of the sea, for he practiced charity all his days.'"

Then Rabbi Akiva spoke up and declared: "Blessed be God, the God of Israel, who hath chosen the words of the Torah and the words of the Sages, for the words of the Torah and the words of the Sages are established forever and unto all eternity. For it is said, (Ecclesiastes 11:1) Send your bread forth upon the waters; for after many days you will find it. Moreover, it is written, (Proverbs 10:2) Tzedakah *saves from death*.[28]

There could not be a more fantastic story than this one of the magical powers of giving *tzedakah*, where even the waves of the ocean rush to the aid of a philanthropic man and deliver him, just in time, from death and then the dissolution of his marriage. According to this way of thinking, one should give *tzedakah*, even if it is a financial hardship, because it will pay off enormous spiritual dividends. As one scholar put it, "Material wealth is for this world. *Tzedakah* is for the soul."[29]

As the belief of heavenly reward was so popular and quoted so often in this context, it is impossible that Maimonides was not aware of it and was not familiar with the belief that the giving of *tzedakah* supernaturally prolongs one's life and saves one from danger. In fact, Maimonides cites other passages from the Babylonian Talmud near these stories. We can then assume that Maimonides deliberately left out references to this belief in his own work on the practice of *tzedakah*.

We can understand why Maimonides left out these tales of the supernatural rewards for practicing *tzedakah* when we remember that Maimonides is a rational philosopher who does not believe in astrology or that one should fulfill a commandment for the sake of a providential reward. For Maimonides, "the Law as a whole aims at two things: the welfare of the soul and the welfare of the body. As for the welfare of the soul, it consists in the multitude's acquiring correct opinions corresponding to their respective capacity... As for the welfare of the

28. *The Fathers According to Rabbi Nathan*, translated by Judah Goldin (New Haven and London: Yale University Press, 1955, 1983) Chapter 3, 30-31.

29. Jacob Neusner, *Tzedakah: Can Jewish Philanthropy Buy Jewish Survival?* (Atlanta: Scholars Press, 1990), 6.

body, it comes about by the improvement of their ways of living one with another."[30]

The law, therefore, teaches people true beliefs and gives civilization its moral integrity. Specifically, the "Laws on Gifts for the Poor" teach society to have "pity for the weak and the wretched, giving strength in various ways to the poor, and inciting us not to press hard upon those in straits and not to afflict the hearts of individuals who are in a weak position."[31] The effects of fulfilling these commandments outside of these purposes, for Maimonides, are irrelevant. Giving *tzedakah*, therefore, may or may not affect one's own situation in life. Maimonides points out, for instance, that one's material wealth or the wealth of one's family can come and go, irrespective of how much charity one has given. "For one who is rich today will be poor tomorrow, or his descendants will be poor; whereas one who is poor today will be rich tomorrow, or his son will be rich."[32] Thus the tales from the Babylonian Talmud or elsewhere about *tzedakah*'s personal rewards in heaven seem to Maimonides to miss the point. A reward is incidental; one's virtue and the dignity of others are of central concern.

The *Mishneh Torah* Compared to the *Guide of the Perplexed*

Although understanding rabbinic literature that preceded Maimonides gives us insight into his philosophy of *tzedakah*, we can understand Maimonides' rationale from the relevant passages he authored in the *Guide of the Perplexed.*

Maimonides' philosophy of *tzedakah* is revealed in a description of the cosmos. In a section dealing with God's providence, we learn that the universe is comprised of a series of powers or spheres, each one in turn exerts its influence on the next until the effects finally reach the earth. The source of this power is God, who, through inexplicable and natural existence, generously overflows to the closest sphere, and then so on through a chain reaction down to the realm of human beings. In an analogy on this point, Maimonides compares the human heart, which Maimonides understood to be the seat of the intellect, to God's role in the universe. Just as the heart governs the body, so does God govern the universe. God is like an inexhaustible and never-diminishing fountain of goodness and wisdom and overflows itself to the farthest reaches. This overflow, for Maimonides, becomes a model for generosity in the practice of *tzedakah.*[33] In his own words, Maimonides says:

---

30. *Guide* III:27, 510.
31. *Guide* III:39, 550-551.
32. *Guide* III:35, 536.
33. *Guide* I:72, 184-194.

> Know that in this comparison that we have established between the world as a whole and a human individual, there is a discrepancy... the ruling part of every living being possessing a heart is profited by the ruled parts; the profit deriving from the latter accrues to it so as to be useful to it. There is nothing like this in the universal being. For to no being, the governance of which overflows or confers a force does any profit accrue in any respect from that which is ruled by it. *For its giving the gifts it gives is like the giving of gifts on the parts of a generous and superior man who does it because of the nobility of his nature and the excellence of his disposition, not because of hope of a reward*: this is to become like the deity, may His name be exalted.[34]

In attempting to compare the generous overflow of God to the universe and the way the rational power of a human being governs the body, Maimonides draws a distinction. God's overflow is utterly and completely giving, and God receives absolutely no benefit from the goodness that pours forth from Him. The heart, however, benefits from a well-managed and healthy body. To illustrate this, we are asked to imagine a human being so noble that generosity naturally occurs to him. He gives of himself because of his nature, not because of some reward. In so doing, he imitates God's generosity.

Maimonides uses this illustration in another part of the *Guide* as well. Maimonides asks us to imagine an

> individual who has enough wealth for a residue to be left over from it sufficient for the enrichment of many people, so that this one may give a measure of it to another individual through which this second would also become rich, while a residue is left over from it that suffices for the enrichment of a third individual. The case of being is similar. For the overflow coming from Him, may He be exalted, for the bringing into being of separate intellects overflows likewise from these intellects, so that one of them brings another one into being.[35]

The distribution of wealth is compared to God's providence over creation. Just as one person enriches another, so does God's influence create intellectual powers that ultimately manifest themselves in the human realm.

---

34. *Guide* I:72, 192. Italics mine.
35. *Guide* II:11, 275.

Furthermore, Maimonides claims at the end and climax of the *Guide* that the ultimate purpose of the law is to enable someone to attain increasing levels of perfection, to raise one up to a level in which one can generously and powerfully affect others. He claims that there are four types of perfection, the first of which is the "perfection of possessions – that is, of what belongs to an individual in the manner of money, garments, tools, slaves, land, and other things of this kind." The second type of perfection is that of "the individual's self, being the perfection of bodily constitution and shape." The next type of perfection that Maimonides claims is higher in value than the previous two is "the perfection of moral virtues. It consists in the individual's moral habits having attained their excellence. Most of the commandments serve no other end than the attainment of this species of perfection." Finally, "the fourth species is the true human perfection; it consists in the acquisition of the rational virtues…this is in true reality the ultimate end; this is what gives an individual true perfection, a perfection belonging to him alone; and it gives him permanent perdurance; through it man is man."[36]

Maimonides, through the tradition of Judaism, would have us all ascend through the levels of perfection to the ultimate state of contemplating God's truth. Through the practice of Jewish law, one ascends against the current of the divine overflow to higher levels of wisdom. The *mitzvot*, by inculcating moral virtues, enable us to make this ascension. Similarly, for Maimonides, the laws pertaining to charity not only have the utilitarian purpose of addressing the problem of the destitute, but they also have the quality of ennobling humanity with virtue. They teach one to become more like God through imitating God's level of generosity. In fact, *tzedakah* is one of the three core values that Maimonides implores us to act upon and imitate in God's likeness along with loving-kindness and judgment.[37] Maimonides is just as concerned with the virtues inculcated into the giver as he is with protecting the vulnerable and giving food to the hungry. Indeed, in the giving of *tzedakah* both the giver and the receiver are lifted up to a higher level of perfection by the practice of charity. The receiver is able to go further along the way toward fulfilling the lower levels of perfection, the perfections of possessions and bodily health, and the giver is ennobled by imitating God's graciousness. Indeed, Maimonides believed, not only as a philosopher but also as a physician, that one cannot seek after God if one is physically deprived or suffering. *Tzedakah* elevates both parties, the giver and the receiver, in the transaction.

In fact, there is a direct link at the conclusion of the *Guide* that ascending in perfection is connected to ascending in giving. Part of the goal in giving *tzedakah* is to overcome material want in society. As one attains wisdom, as well,

---

36. *Guide* III:54, 634-635.
37. *Guide* III:54, 637.

Maimonides claims that one overcomes physical needs. Maimonides addresses this in the context of how the body and its appetites can be an obstacle to the growth of the intellect. He writes,

> The philosophers have already explained that the bodily faculties impede in youth the attainment of most moral virtues, and all the more that of pure thought, which is achieved through the perfection of the intelligibles that lead to passionate love of Him, may He be exalted. For it is impossible that it should be achieved while the bodily humors are in effervescence. Yet in the measure in which the faculties of the body are weakened and the fire of the desires is quenched, the intellect is strengthened, its lights achieve a wider extension, its apprehension is purified, and it rejoices in what it apprehends. The result is that when a perfect man is stricken with years and approaches death, this apprehension increases very powerfully, joy over this apprehension and a great love for the object of apprehension become stronger, until the soul is separated from the body at that moment in this state of pleasure.[38]

Maimonides, here, addresses the process of maturing and approaching death, and as one overcomes the "effervescence" of one's youth, one is able to attain more wisdom. Maimonides also claims, however, that as the body's hold over the mind weakens, the pleasure of wisdom increases. One might conclude, then, that the body's hunger or exposure to the elements, which are consequences of poverty, would create further obstacles in obtaining the path toward perfection. Poverty only increases "the fire of the desires." In providing for someone's physical needs, a giver of *tzedakah* enables another to overcome the body's distracting demands and concentrate on "pure thought."

We can better understand, then, why "Laws on Gifts for the Poor" contains a hierarchy of the kinds of charity in its final and climactic chapter. The eight levels of *tzedakah* reflect the four levels of perfection. Maimonides would like us to ascend through the hierarchy of giving just as he would want us to climb up to higher levels of human perfection. The goal appears to be to become a giving person, whether this means to become someone who gives material sustenance to others or one who overflows with wisdom and governance.

"Laws on Gifts for the Poor," therefore, reflects Maimonides' quest for human perfection as well as the duty to help others on their path towards the contemplation of God's truth. The treatise reflects a philosophy of giving in order

---

38. *Guide* III:54, 627.

to bring oneself and others to a higher state of being. By organizing and explaining these laws, Maimonides is similarly giving to others by sharing his wisdom. The laws are organized in an easy format to understand, and the rationale behind each is explained. Tales of the rewards for the practice of charity are glossed over while Maimonides stresses the benefit and usefulness of the law for civilization. The integrity of Israel depends upon the practice of *tzedakah*, and one's responsibility to one's kin takes on life-saving importance. Ultimately, the virtues of *tzedakah* are preached to the reader, inspiring one to greater moral improvement, climbing to a higher level where one tries to imitate God's ways. We are to ascend to better levels of giving just as we ascend to the highest contemplation of the truth of God.

What follows is an annotated translation of "Laws on Gifts for the Poor." Annotations for Maimonides' sources are included so the reader can compare previous tradition with Maimonides' understanding. Similarly, the criticisms of Ravad are also cited for the reader's interest. While these laws have universal interest, the gender bias of referring to the average Jewish person to whom these laws are applicable as "he" and "him" has been preserved, as has any references to God in the masculine. It is better to understand the original thinking of the sources with their prejudices rather than color them over.

Additional tools, such as a listing of important passages from the Torah, a glossary of technical terms, and a list of the texts and their editions can be found after the translation. All texts were taken from Torah Educational Software Inc., Bar Ilan's Judaic Library Version 5, 1972-1997.

Acknowledgments

Special thanks are due to Dr. Jonathan Cohen and Dr. Barry Kogan of the Hebrew Union College – Jewish Institute of Religion, Rabbi M. Bruce Lustig and Washington Hebrew Congregation, Marcel Bitoun, and Dr. Marc Lee Raphael and the College of William and Mary. Of course, this would not be possible without the love of Rabbi Julie Zupan and Samantha who offer gifts every day.

Maimonides begins the treatise with a list of all of the relevant mitzvot *(divine commandments), dividing them between positive commandments, which are injunctions, and negative commandments, which are prohibitions. All of these are derived directly from the Torah (see the Introduction as well as Appendix I). The first eleven* mitzvot *refer to agricultural produce and are organized in complementary pairs, beginning with an injunction to leave one kind of produce for the poor and a prohibition against taking it. The effort of restraint is matched with the action of giving. The eleventh commandment refers to the tithe for the poor which is part of the system of tithes that the rabbis derived from the Torah.*

The last two mitzvot *deal with giving* tzedakah *in general and apply to an urban scene as well as an agricultural one. They also form a complementary pair, speaking of the action of restraint in not hardening one's heart in one's attitude toward the poor as well as the action of giving generously. Maimonides' list of the commandments is thus clear, organized, and balanced, taking into account the positive and the negative, moving from the literal words of the Torah and the time when Israelites lived in the Land of Israel to the more immediately relevant commandments dealing with his contemporary situation. This list outlines the organization of the entire treatise.*

הלכות מתנות עניים. יש בכללן שלש עשרה מצות, שבע מצות עשה, ושש מצות לא תעשה. וזה הוא פרטן: (א) להניח פאה. (ב) שלא יכלה אותה. (ג) להניח לקט. (ד) שלא ילקט הלקט. (ה) לעזוב עוללות הכרם. (ו) שלא יעולל הכרם. (ז) לעזוב פרט הכרם. (ח) שלא ילקט פרט הכרם. (ט) להניח שכחה. (י) שלא ישוב לקחת השכחה. (יא) להפריש מעשר לעניים. (יב) ליתן צדקה כמסת יד. (יג) שלא יאמץ לבבו על העניים. וביאור מצות אלו בפרקים אלו.

The laws of gifts to the poor. Included in this category are thirteen *mitzvot* [divine commandments], seven positive *mitzvot* [actions that one should do], six negative *mitzvot* [actions that one should not do], and this is how they are individually: 1. To leave the edge of the field. 2. Not to gather it completely. 3. To leave the overlooked gleanings. 4. Not to collect the overlooked gleanings. 5. To leave the malformed grape clusters of the vineyard. 6. Not to strip the vineyard bare. 7. To leave the separated fruit of the vineyard. 8. Not to glean the separated fruit of the vineyard. 9. To leave that which was forgotten. 10. Not to return and take that which was forgotten. 11. To set aside the tithe for the poor. 12. To give as much *tzedakah* [charity] as is within one's power. 13. Not to harden one's heart against the poor. The following chapters contain an explanation of these *mitzvot*.

This chapter provides an overview of the biblical laws of agricultural gifts for the poor. Maimonides begins this introductory chapter by defining produce designated for the poor in a general fashion, and he provides more technical definitions further on as each kind of produce is taken up in turn. Also described here is the process of positive and negative mitzvot *alluded to in the previous list of the relevant commandments to the topic of "gifts for the poor." Specifically, these are all commandments that, if the owner of a field transgresses the prohibition against gathering certain kinds of produce, he may still escape liability by giving from other areas of produce, often to his increased cost.*

The names of the gifts for the poor, given by the rabbis of the Talmud, offer psychological insight into the nature of poverty. They include péah, *indicating the "edge" of the field,* leket, *the "overlooked gleanings,"* peret, *the "separated fruit," principally of grapes,* olélot, *the "malformed grape clusters," and* shikhecha, *the "forgotten" sheaf of the field. It is perhaps no coincidence that the names of the produce given to the poor allude to the kind of people who happen to commonly be poor: those living on the "edge" of society, the "overlooked," the "separated," frequently the "malformed," and often the "forgotten." The names of the produce for the poor remind the giver of the marginalized members of the community.*

הלכה א

הקוצר את שדהו לא יקצור את כל השדה כולה אלא יניח מעט קמה לעניים בסוף השדה שנאמר לא תכלה פאת שדך בקצרך אחד הקוצר ואחד התולש, וזה שמניח הוא הנקרא פאה.

1. One who reaps his field should not reap the whole field entirely but rather he should leave a little bit of standing grain for the poor at the edge of the field, as it is written, (Lev. 23:22) *You shall not reap all the way to the edges of the field.* It is the same whether one is reaping [with a tool] or plucking [by hand], and that which is left is what Scripture refers to as *péah* [the "edge"].

הלכה ב

וכשם שמניח בשדה כך באילנות כשאוסף את פירותיהן מניח מעט לעניים, עבר וקצר את כל השדה או אסף כל פירות האילן לוקח מעט ממה שקצר או ממה שאסף ונותנו לעניים שנתינתו מצות עשה שנאמר לעני ולגר תעזוב אותם, ואפילו טחן הקמה ולשו ואפאו פת הרי זה נותן ממנו פאה לעניים.

2. Just as one must leave [some standing crops] in the field, so too when one gathers the fruit of trees, one should leave a little for the poor. If he does transgress [the negative *mitzvah* against harvesting one's field completely] and reaps all the field or gathers all the trees' fruit, he should take a little from what he reaped or gathered and give it to the poor, for giving it is a positive *mitzvah* [divine commandment], as it is said, (Lev. 23:22) *You shall leave them for the poor and the stranger.* Even if the standing grain is ground, kneaded, and baked

into bread, the one who gives from it is considered to have given *péah* to the poor.[1]

הלכה ג
אבד כל הקציר שקצר או נשרף קודם שנתן הפאה הרי זה לוקה, שהרי עבר על מצות לא תעשה ואינו יכול לקיים עשה שבה שניתק לו.

3. If all of his produce that he reaped was destroyed or burned before he gave *péah*, he deserves punishment [with lashes], for he has transgressed a negative *mitzvah* and cannot fulfill the positive one [to rectify the situation], for the opportunity has been taken from him.[2]

הלכה ד
וכן בלקט כשקוצר ומאלם לא ילקט השבלים הנופלות בשעת הקציר אלא יניחם לעניים שנאמר ולקט קצירך לא תלקט, עבר ולקטן אפילו טחן ואפה נותן לעניים שנאמר לעני ולגר תעזוב אותם, אבדו או נשרפו אחר שלקטן קודם שנתן לעניים לוקה.

4. And so it is with *leket* [overlooked gleanings] as one reaps and binds, one may not gather the fallen stalks at the time of reaping, but rather one should leave them for the poor, as it is said, (Lev. 23:22) *Or gather the gleanings of your harvest.* If one transgresses [the negative *mitzvah* against reaping one's field completely] and reaped them and even kneaded and baked them, one should give them to the poor, as it is said, (Lev. 23:22) *You shall leave them for the poor and the stranger.* If it is destroyed or burned after one has gleaned but before one has given to the poor, one deserves punishment.

הלכה ה
וכן בפרט שנפרט מן הענבים בשעת הבצירה וכן בעוללות שנאמר וכרמך לא תעולל ופרט כרמך לא תלקט לעני ולגר תעזוב אותם, וכן המעמר ושכח אלומה אחת בשדה הרי זה לא יקחנה שנאמר ושכחת עומר בשדה לא תשוב לקחתו, עבר ולקטו אפילו טחנו ואפאו הרי זה נותנו לעניים שנאמר

1. That is, the first part of the verse, (Lev. 23:22) *You shall not reap all the way to the edges of the field,* corresponds to the prohibition against reaping all of the field, and the second part of the verse, *you shall leave them for the poor and the stranger,* corresponds with the injunction to give the food to the poor, no matter what form it is in or how far it has been processed. "Leaving them for the poor and the stranger," therefore, actually indicates actively giving.
2. See Babylonian Talmud Makkot 16b. Punishment, according to the rabbis of the Talmud, usually took the form of lashes, where the offender was whipped across his or her back, based upon Deuteronomy 25:3. Because no one was ever to receive more than forty lashes, the standard number to be received was thirty-nine or less if that is what the offender could bear. Negative commandments were usually punished with lashes while positive commandments were not, but in this case, the commandments not to gather certain agricultural produce involve negative commandments whose transgression could be made up for by fulfilling positive commandments. In this case, it is only when the opportunity to fulfill the positive commandment is also lost and the situation cannot, therefore, be rectified in any fashion that punishment is incurred. This rabbinic understanding of liability also applies to the next two laws.

לגר ליתום ולאלמנה יהיה זו מצות עשה הא למדת שכולן מצות לא תעשה הניתק לעשה הן ואם לא קיים עשה שבהן לוקה.

5. And so it is with *peret* [separated fruit] that fell from the vine at the time of harvesting and with *olélot* [malformed grape clusters], as it is said, (Lev. 19:10) *You shall not pick your vineyard bare [te'olél] or gather the fallen fruit [uferet] of your vineyard; you shall leave them for the poor and the stranger.* So also with one who stacks sheaves and has forgotten a sheaf in the field. This person may not recover it, as it is said, (Deut. 24:19) *And overlook a sheaf in the field, do not turn back to get it.* If one does transgress [the negative *mitzvah* against picking up a forgotten sheaf] and gleans and even grinds and bakes, this one still must give to the poor, as it is said, (Deut. 24:19) *It shall go to the stranger, the fatherless, and the widow*. This is a positive *mitzvah.* Thus you learn that all these *mitzvot* are negative which are transformed into positive *mitzvot*, and if one does not fulfill a positive *mitzvah*, one deserves punishment.[3]

הלכה ו

כשם שהשכחה בעמרים כך היא בקמה, אם שכח מקצת הקמה ולא קצרה הרי זו לעניים, וכשם שהשכחה בתבואה וכיוצא בה כך יש שכחה לאילנות כולן שנאמר כי תחבוט זיתך לא תפאר אחריך והוא הדין לשאר האילנות.

6. Just as it is with forgotten sheaves [*shikhecha*, the "forgotten"], so it is with standing grain. If one has forgotten a portion of standing grain, one may not harvest it. It is for the poor. And just as with forgotten produce and their products, so also with forgotten fruit of trees altogether, as it is said, (Deut. 24:20) *When you beat down the fruit of your olive trees, do not go over them again.* So it applies to all other types of trees.[4]

הלכה ז

נמצאת למד שארבע מתנות לעניים בכרם, הפרט והעוללות והפאה והשכחה, ושלש מתנות בתבואה הלקט והשכחה והפאה, ושתים באילנות השכחה והפאה.

7. Thus we have learned of four gifts to the poor concerning the vineyard: *peret* [the "separated fruit"], *olélot* [the "malformed grape clusters"], *péah* [the "edge"], and *shikhecha* [the "forgotten"]. [We learned] three gifts concerning produce: *leket* [the "overlooked gleanings"], *shikhecha*, and *péah*. And [we learned] two concerning trees: *shikhecha* and *péah*.[5]

---

3. Each one of these verses is two-fold; one part corresponds to the prohibition against gleaning or picking all of a crop while the other part is the injunction to give food to the poor. Each one of the gifts for the poor involves two acts: one of self-restraint and one of giving.
4. With regard to trees, however, there are exceptions, such as with carob trees. See 3:21.
5. See Babylonian Talmud Chullin 131a-b. Maimonides offers a different way of organizing categories of "gifts for the poor," based on applicability. The categories of *peret* and *olélot* apply only to the vineyard while the category of *leket* applies only to the field. *Péah* and *shikhecha* apply to every situation.

הלכה ח
כל מתנות עניים אלו אין בהן טובת הנייה לבעלים, אלא העניים באין ונוטלין אותן על כרחן של בעלים ואפילו עני שבישראל מוציאין אותן מידו.

8. With regard to all of these gifts to the poor, owners may not derive any benefit from them, but rather the poor come and take them regardless of the owner's wishes. Even if he [the farmer] is one of the poor of Israel, they take them from his possession.[6]

הלכה ט
כל גר האמור במתנות עניים אינו אלא גר צדק, שהרי הוא אומר במעשר שני ובא הלוי והגר מה הלוי בן ברית אף הגר בן ברית, ואעפ"כ אין מונעין עניי עכו"ם ממתנות אלו, אלא באין בכלל עניי ישראל ונוטלין אותן מפני דרכי שלום.

9. Any "stranger" that is mentioned [in Scripture] with regards to the gifts for the poor can only refer to a convert, for it states regarding *ma'asér sheni* [the second tithe], (Deut. 14:29) *Then the Levite...and the stranger...shall come.* Just as a Levite is a member of the covenant, so also the stranger is a member of the covenant. Nevertheless, we do not prevent the poor of the Gentiles[7] from these gifts. Rather, they may come along with the poor of Israel and take them for the sake of peaceful relations.[8]

הלכה י
נאמר במתנות עניים לעני ולגר תעזוב אותם כל זמן שהעניים תובעין אותן, פסקו העניים לבקש ולחזר עליהם הרי הנשאר מהן מותר לכל אדם, שאין גופו קדוש כתרומות, ואינו חייב ליתן להן דמיהן שלא נאמר בהן ונתן לעניים אלא תעזוב אותם, ואינו מצווה לעזוב אותן לחיה ולעופות אלא לעניים והרי אין עניים.

10. It is mentioned regarding gifts for the poor, (Lev. 19:10, 23:22) *You shall leave them for the poor and the stranger*, [that is to say] each time the poor have a

---

6. See Babylonian Talmud Chullin 131 a-b. Even if the farmer is poor, he is still obligated to give to the poor as a member of the community. This principle that all may give is taken up again in Chapter 10, with the provision that collectors of *tzedakah* may not cause any public embarrassment to a poor person.
7. Literally, "worshipers of the stars" or idolators.
8. See Mishnah Gittin 5:8, Babylonian Talmud Gittin 61a, and Tosefta Gittin 3:13. Doing something "for the sake of peaceful relations" was ultimately a political reason, where a member of the community would act so as to avoid conflict with others, principally Gentiles. The Jewish community, which was often at the mercy of a hostile ruling power, needed to act so as not to provoke the authorities against them. See later in this treatise in 8:6-8, and also 10:2, where Maimonides states refers to the ruling powers' relationship with the Jews as "the idolatrous nations that hate them and pursue them." It has already been noted in the Introduction that giving to the poor of another ethnic or religious group was remarkable for that time.

claim on them [these gifts], when they have ceased to desire and return after them, the remainder is permitted to anyone, for it is not in and of itself sanctified like gift-offerings [which belong only to the Temple in Jerusalem].[9] Nor is one obligated to give their value's worth, for it does not say, "give them to the poor" but rather *you shall leave them [for the poor]*. It is not a *mitzvah* to leave them for wild animals and birds but rather for the poor, and these [animals] are not "the poor" [but rather they should be used by people].[10]

הלכה יא

מאימתי מותרין כל אדם בלקט, משיכנסו המלקטים שניים וילקטו אחר מלקטים הראשונים ויצאו, מאימתי מותרין כל אדם בפרט ובעוללות משהלכו העניים בכרם ויבואו, הנשאר אחרי כן מותר לכל אדם, מאימתי מותרין כל אדם בשכחה של זיתים, בארץ ישראל אם שכח אותה בראש הזית הרי זה מותר בה מראש חדש כסליו שהוא זמן רביעה שנייה בשנה אפילה, אבל ציבורי זיתים ששכחן תחת האילן הרי זה מותר בהן משיפסקו העניים מלחזר אחריה.

11. When can anyone take *leket*? When the [poor] gleaners come [into the field] a second time and gather after the first group of [poor] gleaners and then depart. When can anyone take *peret* and *olélot*? When the poor have come into the vineyard and gone, what remains after them is permitted to anyone. When can anyone take forgotten olives? In the Land of Israel, if one forgot it [the olive produce] from the top of the olive tree, this is permitted from the first of the month of Kislev, for it is the time of the second rainfall, late in the season. But olives that are left piled up, forgotten under a tree, are permitted [to anyone] as soon as the poor cease from going through them.[11]

הלכה יב

כל זמן שיש לעני ליטול שכחת הזיתים המונחות בארץ תחת האילנות נוטל, ואע"פ שכבר הותר כל אדם בשכחה שבראש האילן, וכל זמן שיש לו ליטול שכחה שבראש האילן נוטל, ואף על פי שעדיין אין לו שכחה תחתיו.

12. Any time that the poor person can take forgotten olives that were left on the ground under the tree, he [the poor person] may take them [that is, it does not depend on the time of the season], even after the time when anyone is permitted to take what was forgotten at the top of the tree. Any time he [anyone] can take forgotten olives that were left on the top of the tree [that is, beginning in Kislev],

9. Giving to the Temple in Jerusalem was a different kind of giving than giving to the poor including any kind of consecrated property or sacrifice, such as a gift-offering. Property became sanctified when the donor said a pledge to that effect and was immediately efficacious, and the use of the property other than for the Temple was prohibited..

10. See Babylonian Talmud 134b, where it says that we leave food for people and not for "ravens and bats."

11. See Mishnah Péah 7:2 and 8:1.

he may take them, even though he still may not take the forgotten olives from beneath the tree that the poor have not yet ceased to go through].[12]

הלכה יג

מתנות עניים שבשדה שאין העניים מקפידים עליהן הרי הן של בעל השדה, ואע״פ שעדיין לא פסקו העניים מלחזור על מתנותיהם.

13. The gifts for the poor that are in the field of which the poor have not claimed belong to the owner, even if the poor have not ceased from going through their gifts.[13]

הלכה יד

כל מתנות העניים האלו אינן נוהגות מן התורה אלא בארץ ישראל כתרומות ומעשרות, הרי הכתוב אומר ובקצרכם את קציר ארצכם כי תקצור קצירך בשדך, וכבר נתפרש בגמרא שהפאה נוהגת בחוצה לארץ מדבריהם, ויראה לי שהוא הדין לשאר מתנות עניים אלו שכולן נוהגות בחוצה לארץ מדבריהם.

14. All of these gifts for the poor as they are in the Torah only apply to the Land of Israel, like gift offerings and tithes. Thus Scripture says, (Lev. 19:9, 23:22) *When you reap the harvest of your land*, [and] (Deut. 24:19) *When you reap the*

12. Maimonides follows an established tradition of dividing a tree in half between top and bottom (see Mishnah Gittin 5:8). The top includes those olives that would need to be beaten down with a stick while the bottom includes those that can be reached by hand. A tree, therefore, cannot be categorized under the requirement of being harvested all at once. In addition, olives left on the ground are like other produce in that, once they have been left behind by their owner, the poor may claim them, and after the poor have gone through them, they are available to anyone. The olives that were not beaten down from the top of the tree, however, depend upon the time of year before they can be considered abandoned by their owner. He bases this upon both Mishnah Péah 7:2 and 8:1. Ravad of Posqiueres, however, takes issue with this, also citing Mishnah Péah 7:2 for a different rule that states that as soon as the olives underneath are deemed to be forgotten so, too, are the olives above. This is reiterated in the Jerusalem Talmud, Péah 7:2, with the added explanation that even if the olives below may be remembered by the owner and not deemed to be forgotten, the olives above are deemed forgotten as soon as the worker has gone through with a harvesting rod and beaten down all that he wanted. In addition, Ravad claims that "underneath" need not only apply to that which is on the ground but actually on the lower branches of the tree, and he also cites the part of a Mishnah that says that if the tree has more than two *seah* of olives on it, then this clearly could not have been forgotten by the owner because it is too large a quantity. Ravad therefore understands that the status of whether or not the olives qualify as *shikhecha* depends entirely upon the actions and intentions of the owner and not the time of year.

13. This passage speaks to the rabbinic understanding of the property of the poor. The poor own these agricultural products and have a claim to them even before the owner of the field has given them because these products are gifts from God and the owner of the field is merely a steward of God's will. It is only when the poor have not claimed the property that it can be understood as being abandoned property and, in that case, the owner of the field or anyone else can take possession of the produce.

harvest in your field. [But] it has already been explained in the Talmud[14] that the category of *péah* applies outside of the Land of Israel from rabbinic law, and it appears to me that it makes sense for the remaining types of gifts for the poor to all apply to outside of the Land of Israel from rabbinic law as well.[15]

הלכה טו

כמה הוא שיעור הפאה, מן התורה אין לה שיעור אפילו הניח שבולת אחת יצא ידי חובתו, אבל מדבריהם אין פחות מאחד מששים בין בארץ בין בחוצה לארץ, ומוסיף על האחד מששים לפי גודל השדה ולפי רוב העניים ולפי ברכת הזרע, כיצד שדה שהיא קטנה ביותר שאם הניח ממנה אחד מששים אינו מועיל לעני הרי זה מוסיף על השיעור, וכן אם היו העניים מרובין מוסיף, ואם זרע מעט ואסף הרבה שהרי נתברך מוסיף לפי הברכה, וכל המוסיף על הפאה מוסיפין לו שכר, ואין לתוספת זאת שיעור.

15. How much is the [minimum] measure of an "edge" portion? From the Torah there is no [minimum] measurement. Even if one left one stalk, one is free from one's obligation, but from rabbinic law it is not less than one-sixtieth whether in the Land of Israel or outside, and one increases over and above one-sixtieth according to the size of the field, the number of poor people, and the blessing of sowing. How so? If a field is exceedingly small and one leaves from it one-sixtieth, it does not benefit a poor person. Thus in this case the measure is increased. And so if there are a great deal of poor people one adds [to the measure], and if the sowing is very little and nevertheless one took in a great deal because one was [unusually] blessed, one increases what one gives according to the abundance of the blessing. Anyone who adds to the measure of the *péah* portion increases his reward [by God], and there is no [maximum] measure to this added benefit.[16]

---

14. See Babylonian Talmud Chullin 137b.
15. See Mishnah Kiddushin 1:9. In this law as well as the next, Maimonides makes a distinction between laws that are from the Torah itself and rabbinic rulings. While laws from the Torah are more directly authoritative, the laws of the rabbis rest on the authority of a tradition of sacred interpretation and were considered just as binding as the laws of the Torah. Indeed, some rabbinic laws carried very severe punishments for their transgression to discourage challenging their authority. The rabbinic law seeks to clarify the intent of the Torah, filling in the gaps that the Torah does not make clear. In this instance, the location of where these laws are in force in the Jewish community and the minimum amount that needed to be given are details lacking in the Torah that the rabbis fill in.
16. See Mishnah Péah 1:1-2. The first line of Mishnah Péah reads, "These are the things for which there is no definite quantity: *péah*, first fruits, the festival offering upon appearing in the Temple, deeds of lovingkindness, and the study of Torah." Taken literally, this means that the Torah does not prescribe a limit in the application of this duty. The implication, however, is that there is no prescribed definite quantity for the reward of following these commandments, as Maimonides makes clear in this law. In addition, one is supposed to be as generous as possible.

The next two chapters deal with the details of the category of péah. *Maimonides, after laying out an overview of the laws of agricultural "gifts for the poor" in the first chapter, now goes back and begins to define and explicate each category one by one.* Péah *is the most general category and thus gets the most scrutiny. Many of the details described here also apply to the other categories of produce. Beginning with the twelfth law, Maimonides makes explicit some of the basic methods of distributing "gifts for the poor" and alludes to the basic rights of both the poor person and the owner of the field.*

הלכה א

כל אוכל שגידוליו מן הארץ ונשמר ולקיטתו כולו כאחת ומכניסין אותו לקיום חייב בפאה, שנאמר ובקצרכם את קציר ארצכם.

1. Anything (1) that people eat, (2) that is raised from the soil, (3) that is supervised, (4) that is gleaned all together at once, and (5) that is put into storage is subject to the giving of the *péah* portion, as it is said, (Lev. 19:9, 23:22) *When you reap the harvest of your land.*[17]

הלכה ב

כל הדומה לקציר בחמש דרכים אלו הוא שחייב בפאה, כגון התבואה והקטניות והחרובין והאגוזין והשקדים והרמונים והענבים והזיתים והתמרים בין יבשים בין רכים וכל כיוצא באלו, אבל אסטיס ופואה וכיוצא בהן פטורין מפני שאינן אוכל, וכן כמהין ופטריות פטורין מפני שאין גידוליהן מן הארץ כשאר פירות הארץ, וכן ההפקר פטור שאין לו מי שישמרנו שהרי הוא מופקר לכל, וכן התאנים פטורין מפני שאין לקיטתן כאחת אלא יש באילן זה מה שיגמר היום ויש בו מה שיגמר לאחר כמה ימים, וכן ירק פטור שאין מכניסין אותו לקיום, השומים והבצלים חייבין בפאה שהרי מייבשין אותן ומכניסין אותן לקיום, וכן האמהות של בצלים שמניחין אותן בארץ ליקח מהן הזרע חייבות בפאה וכן כל כיוצא בהן.

2. Anything to be harvested that shares these five characteristics is liable for the giving of the *péah* portion, such as produce, legumes, carob, nuts, almonds, pomegranates, grapes, olives, dates whether dried or fresh, and such, but woad [a plant that is harvested for blue dye] and rubia [a plant that is harvested for red dye] and similar things are exempt because they are not edible. So also with morils and truffles [which are kinds of mushrooms] because they are not raised from the soil like other produce of the earth. So also is property that has been appropriated by the court ["ownerless property"] exempt, for there is no specific person to supervise it, for it was appropriated for all. So also are figs exempt because they are not picked all at once but rather there are some that are ready on one day and some a few days later. So also are herbs exempt, for they are not put

17. See Mishnah Péah 1:4 as a source for this definition.

into storage. Garlic and onions [however] are liable for giving of *péah*, for people dry them and put them into storage. So also are the shoots of onions liable for the giving of *péah*, for they are put in the ground in order to get their seeds, and so also with similar things.[18]

הלכה ג

קרקע כל שהוא חייבת בפאה ואפילו היתה של שותפין שנאמר קציר ארצכם אפילו של רבים.

3. Cultivated land of any kind is liable for the giving of *péah*, even if it is owned in a partnership, as it is said, (Lev. 19:9, 23:22) *When you reap the harvest of your land*, even if it is land owned by many.

הלכה ד

שדה שקצרו נכרים לעצמן או שקצרוה ליסטים או קרסמוה נמלים או שברתה הרוח או בהמה הרי זו פטורה מן הפאה, שחובת הפאה בקמה.

4. A field that was harvested by Gentiles for themselves, or one that was harvested by bandits, or one that was chewed down by ants,[19] or one that was laid low by the wind or cattle is exempt from the giving of *péah*, for the obligation of *péah* is on things still standing.[20]

הלכה ה

קצר חציה וקצרו הליסטים חציה שנשאר הרי זו פטורה, שהחיוב בחצי שקצרו הליסטים אבל אם קצרו הליסטים חציה וחזר הוא וקצר השאר נותן פאה כשיעור מה שקצר, קצר חציה ומכר חציה הלוקח נותן פאה)לכל(, קצר חציה והקדיש חציה הפודה מיד הגזבר נותן פאה לכל, קצר חציה והקדישו מניח מן הנשאר פאה הראויה לכל.

5. One who harvested half [of his field] and then bandits harvested the other half that remained is exempt [from giving *péah*], for the obligation was to come from the half that the bandits harvested. But if the bandits harvested half and then the owner came back and harvested the remaining half, he gives *péah* according to the measure of what he harvested. If he harvested [the first] half and sold [the second] half, the one who took [what he sold] gives *péah* (for all). If he harvested [the first] half and dedicated [the second] half to the Temple, the redeemer, [who

---

18. See Mishnah Péah 1:4-5. Maimonides adds a great deal to the Mishnah, but he follows the same principle: food for the poor included basic kinds of food that were processed in the usual way under regular processes and supervision. In addition, the food also needed to be able to be conserved for future consumption as a matter of practical interest and to avoid waste. Luxury items, such as figs and herbs, which required special care, were exempt, but garlic and onions, which do not require special care and can be harvested like a regular crop, are not. It is also interesting to note that the principle of conservation also extends to the shoots of onions, implying that the poor might participate in the processes of planting and harvesting on land of their own.

19. Some texts read גמלים, "camels," but as this is based upon Mishnah Péah 2:7, "ants" is what was intended.

20. However, see law 2:10 of this chapter where the Gentiles are not robbers but hired workers.

takes it] from the possession of the treasurer, gives *péah* for all.[21] If he harvested [the first] half and redeemed it, he leaves *péah* from what remains as is appropriate for all of the crop.

הלכה ו

כרם שהיה בוצר ממנו ענבים למכור בשוק ובדעתו שיניח השאר לגת לדרוך אותו, אם היה בוצר לשוק מכאן ומכאן הרי זה נותן פאה למה שבוצר לגת כפי הנשאר, ואם היה בוצר לשוק מרוח אחת מלבד הרי זה נותן פאה מן הנשאר כפי הראוי לכל הכרם הואיל ובצר מרוח אחת אינו כבוצר עראי מעט מכאן ומעט מכאן שהוא פטור, וכן כל הקוטף מלילות מעט מעט ומכניס לביתו אפילו קטף כן כל שדהו פטור מן הלקט ומן השכחה ומן הפאה.

6. In the case of a grape-harvester who has a field from which he takes grapes to sell in the market and the remainder he intends to leave for the wine press, if the grape-harvester took the grapes to the market a bit from here and a bit from there, then the grape-harvester gives *péah* from what he left for the wine press according to the measure of what was left. But if the grape-harvester took the grapes to the market all from one side of his field, then he should give *péah* from the remaining grapes according to the measure of the entire vineyard because one who harvests grapes all from one side of his field is not like a grape-harvester who by chance takes a little bit from here and a little bit from there, who, in that case, is exempt. So also this applies to one who plucks parched ears of corn bit by bit and brings them into his house.[22] Even if he plucks his entire field this way, he is exempt from *leket*, *shikhecha*, and *péah*.[23]

הלכה ז

הקוצר כל שדהו קודם שתוגמר ועדיין לא הביאה שליש הרי זו פטורה, ואם הגיעה לשליש חייבת, וכן בפירות האילן אם נגמרו שליש גמירתן חייבין.

7. One who harvests his field before it has ripened, that is, it has not yet ripened one-third of the way, it [this field] is exempt, but if it was one-third of the way ripened, it [the field's produce] is subject to *péah*. So also with the fruit of trees that if it is one-third of the way ripened, it [the fruit] is subject to *péah*.

הלכה ח

המקדיש שדהו והיא קמה חייבת בפאה, קצרה הגזבר ואחר כך פדאה פטורה, שבשעת חיוב הפאה היתה קודש שאינו חייב בפאה.

8. One who sanctifies corn [and redeems it] while it is still standing [and not yet harvested] owes *péah*. If the treasurer harvested it and afterwards he [the owner] redeemed it, it is exempt, for at the time of the obligation of *péah* the crop was sanctified and [therefore] he does not owe *péah*.[24]

---

21. See Mishnah Péah 2:7-8. There is no *péah* obligation for anything dedicated to the Temple.
22. This is apparently different because this is for consumption in the home.
23. The fourth qualification was that produce be gleaned all at once, like an ordinary crop, and not like a home garden for personal consumption. These instances present ambiguities in this area.
24. See Mishnah Péah 4:7.

הלכה ט
נכרי שקצר שדהו ואחר כך נתגייר הרי זו פטור מן הפאה ומן הלקט ומן השכחה אע"פ שאין השכחה אלא בשעת העימור.

9. A Gentile who harvested his field and afterwards converted is exempt from *péah*, *leket*, and *shikhecha*, even though *shikhecha* can only be owed during the time of carrying the sheaves home [when he would have been considered a Jew].[25]

הלכה י
אין שוכרין פועלים נכרים לקצור מפני שאינן בקיאין בלקט ופאה, ואם שכר וקצרו את כולו הרי זו חייבת בפאה.

10. One should not hire Gentile workers for harvesting because they are not familiar with the laws of *leket* and *péah*, but if one hired them and they harvested everything, then the owner still owes *péah*.[26]

הלכה יא
בעל הבית שקצר כל שדהו ולא הניח פאה, הרי זה נותן מן השבלים פאה לעניים, ואינו צריך לעשר, ואם נתן להם רוב הקציר משום פאה הרי זה פטור מן המעשרות, וכן אם דש ועדיין לא זרה נותן להם הפאה קודם שיעשר, אבל דש וזרה ברחת ובמזרה וגמר מלאכתו מעשר ונותן להם מן הפירות המעושרין שיעור הפאה הראויה לאותה שדה, וכן באילנות.

11. A landowner who harvested his field and did not leave *péah* should give *péah* from the harvested sheaves to the poor, and he does not need to tithe it. And if he gave them the majority of his harvest in the name of giving *péah*, he is exempt from tithes. So also this applies if he threshed his produce but still did not bundle it, he must give *péah* before he has tithed. But if he threshed and bundled with a winnowing shovel and a winnowing fan and thus finished all of his labor, he tithes and then gives [*péah*] to them from the tithed produce according to the measure of what is fitting for that field. So also does this apply to produce from trees.[27]

For the remainder of the chapter, Maimonides addresses what might be termed the "constitutional" rights of both the owner of the field and the poor person in that these rights are believed to be given by God. The assumption underlying all of the gifts for the poor is that these are God's gifts to the poor and not the gifts of the owner of the field. Therefore, the poor have a claim to certain kinds of produce even before the owner of the field physically gives it to them.

---

25. See Mishnah Péah 4:6.
26. See Tosefta Péah 3:1.
27. See Mishnah Péah 1:6. While the situations described here are different from that of the Mishnah, the ideas seem to be related. The system of tithes is described in Chapter 6. See also Babylonian Talmud Bava Kama 94a.

The poor are entitled to be fed because, according to this thinking, God has given them this food, and the owner of the field is God's steward in this transaction. The owner of the field must perform this duty in as transparent and easy a fashion as possible, free of deception or intimidation, no matter how tempting the produce or its profits might be. If the owner of the field fails in this duty of giving the poor their due, he has essentially stolen another's property (see below in 4:10). On the other hand, just as the poor have a right to certain kinds of food, the owner of the field has the right to designate and transfer this property. The relationship of both parties, the owner of the field and the poor person, is determined by their relationship to God, and it is God who has the ultimate authority in giving out the land and its produce to whomever God wishes.

הלכה יב
אין מניחין את הפאה אלא בסוף השדה, כדי שיהיו עניים יודעין מקום שיבאו לו וכדי שתהיה ניכרת לעוברים ולשבים ולא יחשד, ומפני הרמאים שלא יתכוין לקצור הכל ואומר לאלו שרואים אותו קוצר סוף השדה בתחלת השדה הנחתי, ועוד שלא ישמור שעה שאין שם אדם ויניחנה ויתננה לעני הקרוב לו, עבר והניח הפאה בתחלת השדה או באמצעה הרי זו פאה, וצריך שיניח בסוף השדה כשיעור הפאה הראויה למה שנשאר בשדה אחר שהפריש את הראשונה.

12. One should only leave *péah* from the end of one's field so that the poor know the place they are to go and so that it is known to the passers-by, so they will not suspect anything. This is so because there are liars who intend to harvest the whole field who could say to those who see him harvesting the end of the field, "I left my due from the beginning of the field." And moreover [this applies so] he will not wait until a time when no one is around and leaves [his due] to his poor relative. But, if he transgressed and left *péah* from the beginning of the field or from the middle, this still counts toward [the total amount of] the *péah* portion. However, he still needs to leave the rest [of his due] from the end of the field so as to fulfill the fitting measure of *péah* after he has separated the first part.[28]

הלכה יג
בעל הבית שנתן פאה לעניים ואמרו לו תן לנו מצד זה ונתן להם מצד אחר זו וזו פאה, וכן בעל השדה שהפריש פאה ואמר הרי זו פאה וגם זו או שאמר הרי זו פאה וזו הרי שתיהן פאה.

13. A landowner who gave *péah* from one side to the poor, and they say to him, "Give to us from that side," and he gave to them from that other side, both portions count as *péah*. So also with a landowner who separates his portion for

28. See Tosefta Péah 1:7 and Babylonian Talmud Shabbat 23a-b. This law speaks to the transparency of the system of giving to the poor and fighting corruption. Also illustrated here is a principle of what should be in theory versus accepting something not scrupulously done after the fact.

péah and said, "This is *péah* and so also is this," or he said, "This is *péah* and this;" both of them count toward the *péah* portion.[29]

הלכה יד

אסור לפועלים לקצור את כל השדה אלא מניחין בסוף השדה כשיעור הפאה, ואין לעניים בה כלום עד שיפרישנה בעל הבית מדעתו, לפיכך עני שראה פאה בסוף שדה אסור ליגע בה משום גזל עד שיודע לו שהיא מדעת בעל הבית.

14. It is forbidden for workers to harvest all of a field unless they leave at the end of the field the appropriate area for giving *péah*, and nothing is given to the poor at all until the landowner separates it for that purpose in full knowledge. Therefore, for a poor person who sees *péah* at the end of the field, it is forbidden for him to labor in it because it would be considered as theft until he knows for certain that this is the intention of the owner.[30]

הלכה טו

הפאה של תבואה וקטניות וכיוצא בהן מזרעים הנקצרים, וכן פאת הכרם והאילנות ניתנת במחובר לקרקע והעניים בוזזין אותה בידם, ואין קוצרין אותה במגלות ואין עוקרין אותו בקרדומות כדי שלא יכו איש את רעהו, רצו העניים לחלקה ביניהם הרי אלו מחלקין, אפילו תשעים ותשעה אומרין לחלק ואחד אומר לבוז לזה האחד שומעין שאמר כהלכה.

15. The *péah* portion of grain, legumes, and similar plants that are harvested, and so also with the *péah* portions of the vineyard and the trees, [the produce of] which is directly connected to the ground which the poor must pull up with their hands, they [the poor] may not harvest them with scythes and may not uproot them with spades so that one does not strike another. If the poor people want to divide up the produce among them [rather than on a first-come, first-serve basis by pulling with their hands] then they may divide it up, but if ninety-nine [out of a hundred] say to divide it and one says to pull it up with their hands [on a first-come, first-serve basis], they heed the one, for he spoke according to the law.[31]

הלכה טז

פאה של דלית ושל דקל שאין עניים מגיעין לבוז אותה אלא בסכנה גדולה, בעל הבית מוריד אותה ומחלק אותה בין העניים, ואם רצו כולן לבוז אותה לעצמן בוזזין, אפילו תשעים ותשעה אומרים לבוז ואחד אומר לחלק שומעין לאחד שאמר כהלכה ומחייבין בעל הבית להוריד ולחלק ביניהן.

16. In the case of the *péah* portion that is given from suspended vines[32] or from

---

29. See Tosefta Péah 2:6.

30. See Tosefta Péah 2:7-8.

31. See Mishnah Péah 4:1-2, 4. Violence among the poor was obviously a concern as they fought for food.

32. A suspended vine is also known as a trained vine because it is trained to grow in a certain direction and suspended up high.

date palm trees [that are up high] that the poor cannot reach to pick without great risk, the landowner must bring the food down and divide it up evenly among the poor people. If they want to [go up and] pick it themselves, they may do so. But even if ninety-nine [out of a hundred] say to pick them and one says to divide them, they heed the one, for he spoke according to the law, and the landowner is obligated to bring the produce down and divide it among them.[33]

הלכה יז

בשלש עתות ביום מחלקין את הפאה לעניים בשדה או מניחין אותם לבוז, בשחר, ובחצי היום, ובמנחה, ועני שבא שלא בזמן זה אין מניחין אותו ליטול, כדי שיהיה עת קבוע לעניים שיתקבצו בו כולן ליטול, ולמה לא קבעו לה עת אחת ביום מפני שיש שם עניות מניקות שצריכות לאכול בתחלת היום, ויש שם עניים קטנים שאין נעורין בבקר ולא יגיעו לשדה עד חצי היום, ויש שם זקנים שאינם מגיעין עד המנחה.

17. At three times of the day they divide up the *péah* portion in the field for the poor or leave it for them to pick: at dawn, at noon, and at *mincha*,[34] and they do not leave anything for the poor person who does not come at these times so that there is a set time for the poor to gather together and take [what they need]. Why was there not only one set time during the day? Because there are nursing mothers who are poor who need to eat at the beginning of the day, there are poor children who do not stir during the morning and do not arrive to the field until noon, and there are old people who cannot arrive until *mincha*.[35]

הלכה יח

עני שנטל מקצת הפאה וזרק על השאר או שנפל עליה או שפירש טליתו עליה קונסין אותו ומעבירין אותו ממנה ואפילו מה שנטל לוקחין אותו מידו וינתן לעני אחר]וכן בלקט וכן בעומר השכחה[.

18. If a poor person takes his portion of *péah* and throws something on the remainder, falls on it, or spreads out his garment on it [as an act of claiming it], they fine him and take him away and they even confiscate what he took from him and give it to another poor person. So also with *leket* and so with *shikhecha*.[36]

הלכה יט

מי שלקח את הפאה ואמר הרי זה לאיש פלוני העני, אם עני הוא זה שלקח מתוך שזוכה בו לעצמו זכה בו לאותו פלוני, ואם עשיר הוא לא זכה לו אלא יתננה לעני שנמצא ראשון.

---

33. See Mishnah Péah 4:1-2, 4. In both this and the previous passage, there is a conflict with what might be easier and even more reasonable versus the literal letter of the law. Because the law is understood to be holy, there must be unanimous consensus to accomplish the goal of distributing this produce in a fashion different from the literal method.

34. Late afternoon.

35. See Mishnah Péah 4:5.

36. See Mishnah Péah 4:3.

19. If someone took the *péah* portion and said, "This is for so-and-so, who is poor," if he [the taker] is poor, then he can take it on his own merit and thus have it for so-and-so, but if he [the taker] is a wealthy person, he may not have it, but rather he must give it to the next poor person who appears.[37]

הלכה כ

בעל הבית שהניח פאה לעניים אלו העומדים לפניו ובא עני אחר מאחוריו ונטלה זכה בה שאין אדם זוכה בלקט שכחה ופאה וסלע של מציאה עד שיגיע לידו.

20. When a landowner leaves *péah* for those poor people who stand [in a line] before him, and another poor person comes up behind him and takes from it [the pile of produce to be given out], he [the poor person] may keep it [even though he acquired it unfairly], for no one possesses *leket* or *shikhecha* or *péah* or even a coin that was found until it is in his hand [and without possession those standing in line have no legal claim to it as their property].[38]

37. See Mishnah Péah 4:9.
38. See Tosefta Péah 2:2.

Maimonides continues to explicate the laws of péah, *focusing on the task of defining what constitutes a "field," things that may or may not divide a field, and the complications of joint ownership and liability. Maimonides also applies the laws of* péah *to different kinds of orchards.*

הלכה א
אין מניחין את הפאה משדה על חברתה כיצד, היו לו שתי שדות לא יקצר את האחת כולה ויניח בשניה פאה הראויה לשתיהן, שנאמר לא תכלה פאת שדך בקוצרך שיניח בכל אחת ואחת פאה הראויה לה, ואם הניח משדה על חברתה אינה פאה.

1. One does not leave *péah* for one field from another field. How so? If a farmer had two fields, he may not harvest one entirely and leave *péah* of the second one in proportion for both of them, as it is said, (Lev. 23:22) *You shall not reap all the way to the end of your field* [singular]. He should leave *péah* of each and every field as is fitting for it. If he leaves [*péah*] for one field from another, this does not count as leaving *péah.*

הלכה ב
היתה שדהו זרועה כולה מין אחד והיה נחל בתוך השדה אע"פ שאינו מושך או אמת המים שאינו יכול לקצור מה שבשני צדדיה כאחת והוא שתהיה מושכת וקבועה, הרי זה כשתי שדות ונותן פאה מצד זה לעצמו ומצד זה לעצמו.

2. If one has a field that is sown all with one type of crop and a river flows through the field, even though it may not be flowing [that is, it is a stagnant body of water], or it is [merely] a channel of water so wide that one cannot harvest what is on both sides all together and the channel is continuous and permanent, then this is as if there are two fields and one gives *péah* from one for itself and the other for itself.[39]

הלכה ג
וכן אם היה מפסיק דרך היחיד שהוא רחב ארבע אמות או דרך הרבים הרחב שש עשרה אמה אבל שביל היחיד והוא פחות מארבע או שביל הרבים פחות משש עשרה אמה אם היה קבוע בימות החמה ובימות הגשמים מפסיק, ואם אינו קבוע בימות הגשמים אינו מפסיק אלא הרי הוא כשדה אחת.

3. So also a private road that is at least four cubits wide or a public road that is at least sixteen cubits wide form a partition [between the two parts of the field]. In the case of a private path which is less than four cubits[40] or a public path that is

39. For this law through number seven of this chapter, see Mishnah Péah 2:1-2. Water always divides a field into two because one cannot harvest the crop all together.

40. Ravad objects saying that a private path must be at least four cubits wide in all cases in order to form a partition, otherwise it may merely serve as access between vineyards and fields and not really a road for those passing through.

less than sixteen cubits, if it is in regular use during both the dry and the rainy season, then it forms a partition, but if it is not in regular use during the rainy season, it does not count as a partition, and this is considered to be one field [all year round].[41]

הלכה ד

היה מפסיק בה ארץ בורה שאינו זרועה ולא חרושה, או ארץ נירה והיא שנחרשה ולא נזרעה, או שהפסיק בה זרע אחר, כגון שהיה חטים מכאן וחטים מכאן ושעורים באמצע, או שקצר באמצעה אפילו קודם שתביא שליש וחרש מקום שקצר, הרי זה נפסקת לשתי שדות, והוא שיהיה רוחב כל אחד מאלו כשלשה תלמים של פתיח והוא פחות מבית רובע, במה דברים אמורים בשדה קטנה שהיא חמשים אמה של שתי אמות או פחות, אבל אם היתה יתרה על זו אין הבור או הניר מפסיקה לשתים אלא א"כ היתה בו רוחב בית רובע, אבל זרע אחר כל שהוא מפסיק בה.

4. In the case of a field that is divided by fallow land which is not sown or ploughed, or land that is broken up and ploughed but not sown, or land planted with different kinds of crops, such as wheat on either side and barley in the middle, or if one harvested the middle, even if it was before the crop became a third of the way ripe and he ploughed the area he harvested, then this area is divided into two fields. This is in the case of each field [on either side] being at least the width of three furrows of ploughed land, which is a little less than an amount of land required to plant one-fourth of a *kav* of seed. How does this apply? This pertains to a small field that is fifty cubits by two cubits or less [that one is dividing into even smaller fields], but if it is more, the fallow land or broken land does not form a partition dividing the field into two unless it [the divider] is the width of the amount of land required for one-fourth of a *kav* of

41. In other words, year-round used paths that are less than the minimum width constitute a partition between the fields, but paths not used part of the year do not constitute a partition. See Mishnah Bava Batra 6:7.

seed.[42] In the case, however, of a different kind of crop going down the middle, any quantity of land serves as a partition.

הלכה ה

אכלה גובאי או קרסמוה נמלים באמצעה אם חרש מקום שאכלו הרי זה מפסיק.

5. If locusts consumed [the crop] or ants devoured it down the middle, if the farmer ploughs the land that they ate, then this forms a partition [and each side is considered a separate field].[43]

הלכה ו

הזורע בהר שאינו כולו שוה אלא יש בו תילים גבוהים ומקומות מקומות עמוקות אע"פ שאינו יכול לחרוש אותו כולו ולזרעו כאחת אלא נחרש המקום הגבוה בפני עצמו והנמוך בפני עצמו הרי זה כשדה אחת ומניח פאה אחת בסוף ההר על כל ההר.

6. One who plants on a land with hills so that the entirety of it [the field] is uneven, so there are peaks and valleys, even though one is unable to plough it entirely and to sow it as one but harvests the peaks by themselves and the valleys by themselves, then this is [still] considered to be one field, and one leaves *péah* for the field at the end of the hilly region for all the hills.

הלכה ז

מדרגות שהן גבוהות עשרה טפחים נותן פאה מכל אחת ואחת, ואם היו ראשי שורות מעורבים נותן מאחת על הכל, היו פחות מעשרה אע"פ שאין ראשי השורות מעורבין נותן מאחת על הכל, היה סלע על פני כל השדה, אם עוקר הוא את המחרישה מצד זה ונותנה מצד זה מפסיק, ואם לאו אינו מפסיק.

---

42. Maimonides claims that if one has a small, narrow field and wants to divide it into two even smaller fields, if one leaves a portion of uncultivated or simply ploughed land in between two parts of this thin field, then this serves as an adequate partition so long as the two parts are at least three furrows wide and can still be considered a field each in its own right. If, however, the field is not long and thin but larger, the divider itself must be larger, at least as large as an area in which a quarter of a *kav* of seed might be sown (approximately 100 square cubits). Ravad, however, points out that this is not in accordance with what is written in the Jerusalem Talmud Péah 2:1. There it describes two approaches to dividing a field with fallow or ploughed land. In that source, the sage Rav says that a field may be divided by a section of land large enough to require a quarter of a *kav* of seed, while Rabbi Yochanan says that the divider need only be three furrows in width. The Talmud goes on to explain that these approaches do not contradict each other, only that Rav defines the divider in terms of total area while Yochanan defines the divider in terms of width, and one could say that a divider of three furrows width is fifty cubits by two cubits, thereby satisfying Rav's measurement. Ravad clarifies that Rav's approach easily pertains when dealing with a very large field, that if one has a square section of 100 square cubits or more of uncultivated or ploughed land in the middle of a very large field, then this can serve as a divider. Yochanan's approach is applicable to the more common scenario of having either a large or a small field where one has a thin strip of land dividing it. Ravad's implication is that Maimonides has confused which measurement goes with which field, that the long, thin field that is fifty by two cubits is the divider and not the total field.

43. See Tosefta Péah 1:8.

7. If the land forms steps and they are ten handsbreadths high,[44] one leaves *péah* for each and every terrace, but if the beginnings of the rows are mixed together [and then the land separates into steps], one gives from one level for the entire area. If they are less then ten handsbreadths high, regardless of whether the beginnings of the roads are mixed together, one gives from one level for the entire area. If there is a rock that runs through the entire field, if one has to unhitch the plough [from behind the animal in order to get the plough] from one side of the rock over to the other side, then this forms a partition, but if it does not [jut out this way] then it does not form a partition.[45]

הלכה ח

הזורע שדה שיש בה אילנות אע"פ שהיא מלבנות מלבנות בין האילנות ואין כל הזרע מעורב נותן פאה אחת לכל השדה, שדבר ידוע ששדה אחת היא ומפני מקום האילנות נחלק הזרע.

8. If one sows a field in which there are trees, even if there are plots of land between the trees but the crops are not mixed in between, one gives *péah* from one section for the entire field, for it is obvious that this is a single field but because of the location of the trees, the crop was divided.[46]

הלכה ט

במה דברים אמורים בשהיו האילנות כל עשרה בתוך בית סאה, אבל אם היו כל עשרה אילנות ביותר מבית סאה הרי זה נותן פאה מכל מלבן ומלבן, שהרי האילנות מרוחקים הרבה ולא מפני האילנות זרע מלבנות מלבנות.

9. In what situation does this apply? When there are ten trees on an amount of land large enough for one *séah* of seed, but if among ten trees one can sow more than a *séah* of seed, then one gives *péah* for each and every plot, for the trees are spread out and it is not because of the trees that the crop is in different plots.[47]

---

44. In agriculture, this is a common terrace. The land is cultivated to look like large steps down a hillside.

45. See Tosefta Péah 1:12.

46. See Mishnah Péah 3:1.

47. The issue here is whether or not trees can act as dividers that same way rivers can. Maimonides claims that it depends on the density of the number of trees on the land. Citing Mishnah Péah 3:1 and the Jerusalem Talmud Péah 3:1, Ravad objects that this is not the approach of the sages. In fact, there is a dispute between the Schools of Hillel and Shammai on this point. Those of Hillel state that a plot of land with grain sown in between trees is treated as one field, while Shammai say that the trees act as dividers and the grain in between the trees is divided into separate plots. However, both acknowledge that if the trees are scattered so there is a large space for the grain in between the trees, this is treated as one field, and if there are many trees in a small space, then the trees act as a divider. The point of disagreement comes with the measure of ten trees on an amount of land large enough for one *séah* seed. Those of Hillel seem to say that this is treated as one field, while those of Shammai say that this is sufficient for a divider. Maimonides follows the rule of Hillel. Ravad, however, states that the Jerusalem Talmud teaches us that the formation of the trees determines

הלכה י
וכן מלבנות הבצלים שבין הירק נותן פאה אחת לכל הבצלים, ואף על פי שהירק מבדיל ביניהן ומשימם מלבנות מלבנות.

10. So also with plots of onions, that between vegetables one gives *péah* for all the onions, even if the vegetables form divisions between them and one places them in different plots.[48]

הלכה יא
שדה שכולה זרועה מין אחד וכיון שהתחילו בה מקומות ליבש עקר או תלש מה שיבש מכאן ומכאן עד שנשאר הלח מפורד מלבנות מלבנות מרוחקות זו מזו, אם היה דרך בני אדם שם לזרוע מאותו המין ערוגות ערוגות כגון שבת או חרדל הרי זה מניח פאה מכל מלבן ומלבן, שהרואה אומר ערוגות ערוגות נזרעו, ואם היה מין אחד שזורעין אותו שדות כגון תבואה וקטניות נותן אחת לכל.

11. In the case of a field that is sown entirely with one type of crop, when certain patches of it begin to dry [and ripen] and [the farmer] uproots and plucks what has dried from here and there leaving the fresh [unripe] crop in separate patches far from each other [so that they appear like separate fields], if this is the usual way for people to sow this kind of crop in separate beds, such as dill or mustard, then he should leave *péah* from each and every plot, for anyone who sees would say that they were sown in beds.[49] But if this is the kind of crop that people sow in fields, such as grain or legumes, then he gives *péah* from one patch for the whole crop.

הלכה יב
במה דברים אמורים כשהיה יבש מכאן ויבש מכאן ולח באמצע, אבל לח מכאן ומכאן ויבש באמצע מניח מן היבש בפני עצמו ומן הלח בפני עצמו.

12. In what situation does this apply? When there is dried [ripe] crop on either side and fresh [unripe] crop in between, but if the fresh [unripe] crop is here and there and the dry [ripe] crop is in between, one leaves [*péah*] from the dried [ripe] crop for itself and from the fresh [unripe] crop for itself separately.[50]

---

the law. If the ten trees on land sufficient for one *séah* of land are close together, then they form a divider, but if they are scattered, then we should follow the rule of Hillel and treat it as one field.

48. See Mishnah Péah 3:4.

49. See Mishnah Péah 3:2.

50. Ravad objects strongly, saying that Maimonides has confused two separate, albeit similar, subjects, and Maimonides does not rule in accordance with Jewish law. According to Ravad, Maimonides has confused the law of what happens when one reaps the ripe portion of a field down the middle and thereby creates two separate fields of unripe grain on either side (as taught by Rabbi Akiva in Mishnah Péah 3:2) with the issue of a farmer who plucks casually from here and there in his field and thereby leaves patches behind. As expounded in the Jerusalem Talmud Péah 3:2 attributed to Rabbi Meir in accordance with Rabbi Akiva, if one

הלכה יג
שדה שזרעה בצלים או פולים או אפונים וכיוצא בהן והיה בדעתו למכור מקצתן לחין בשוק ומניח מקצת השדה יבש ויעשה ממנו גורן, חייב להניח פאה לזה שמוכר לח בפני עצמו ולזה שקוצר אותו יבש בפני עצמו.

13. In the case of a field sown with onions, beans, peas, or similar items, if one's intention was to sell part of it fresh in the market and leave part of it to dry for storage, one is obligated to leave *péah* for that which one sells fresh separately from that which one harvests dry.[51]

הלכה יד
הזורע את שדהו מין אחד אע"פ שהוא עושהו שתי גרנות מניח פאה אחת, זרעה שני מינים אף על פי שהוא עושה אותה גורן אחת נותן פאה למין זה בפני עצמו ופאה למין זה בפני עצמו.

14. If one who sows his field with one type of crop, even if he can make two store-chambers[52] out of it, he leaves *péah* for it as one unit. If he sowed two types of crops, even if he can only make one store-chamber out of it, he gives *péah* for each type of crop separately.[53]

הלכה טו
זרע שני זרעים ממין אחד כגון שזרעה שני מיני חטים או שני מיני שעורים, אם עשאן גורן אחת נותן פאה אחת שתי גרנות נותן שתי פאות ודבר זה הלכה למשה מסיני.

15. If one sowed two types of seed for one kind of crop, such as having sowed two types of wheat or two types of barley, if one makes one store-chamber out of it, then he should give *péah* for it as one unit. If he makes two store-chambers, then he should give two portions of *péah* [one from each]. This is the law of Moses at Sinai.[54]

---

reaps a ripe portion of a field and in doing so divides a field in half so that the unripe portions are no longer continuous, then one treats these as separate fields and gives *péah* from each. The law, according to Ravad, only addresses the issue of crops that remain after such a reaping. The Jerusalem Talmud here does not say anything about the case of a farmer plucking from here and there. We do not know what Rabbi Meir would have said in such a case, although the sages rule in accordance with what Maimonides has written, namely, that one who casually reaps in patches gives *péah* from the whole as one field. Ultimately, Ravad's objection is that Maimonides has oversimplified matters.

51. See Mishnah Péah 3:3.

52. "Store-chamber" is one definition and is used here for the sake of consistency and known to the common reader. "Threshing floor" is another definition and may be more precise in this context.

53. See the first part of Mishnah Péah 2:5.

54. See Mishnah Péah 2:5-6. The expression "the law of Moses at Sinai" indicates an established tradition not derived explicitly from the Torah.

הלכה טז
האחין שחלקו נותנין שתי פאות, חזרו ונשתתפו נותנין פאה אחת, השותפין שקצרו חצי השדה ואחר כך חלקו, זה שלקח הקציר אינו מפריש כלום, וזה שלקח הקמה מפריש על החצי שלקח בלבד, חזרו ונשתתפו וקצרו החצי האחר בשותפות, כל אחד מהן מפריש מחלקו שבקמה על חלק חבירו שבקמה אבל לא על החצי שנקצר.

16. Brothers [who are business partners, probably because of their inheritance] who separate [and dissolve their partnership] need to give two portions of *péah* [one apiece]. If they come back together as partners, they give one portion of *péah*. If partners harvest half of a field and then separate, the one who took the harvested portion does not set aside anything [for *péah*], and the one who took the standing grain sets aside [*péah*] for the half he took alone.[55] If they came back and became partners again, and harvested the other half in their partnership, each of them sets aside [*péah*] from his portion of standing grain over against the portion of his partner's standing grain, but he does not [set aside *péah*] over the portion that was previously harvested.[56]

הלכה יז
שדה שהגיע חציה עד שליש וחציה לא הגיע, והתחיל וקצר בחצי שהגיע חציו ואחר כך הביאה כולה שליש ואחר כך גמר החצי הראשון שהגיע בתחלה, מפריש מן הראשון על האמצעיים ומן האמצעיים על הראשון ועל האחרון.

17. In the case of a field, half of which became one-third of the way ripe and half of which did not, so he [the farmer] began to harvest the half which had begun to ripen and completed harvesting only that half. Then after some time the whole remaining part of the field [that was not ripe at all] became one-third of the way ripe and then he completed harvesting the first part. He should then set aside *péah* from the first section on the intermediate section [that is, for the first section that he harvested, he sets aside *péah* for the whole first half of the field that had become one-third of the way ripe] and on the intermediate section from the first and the last [that is, on the second half that became one-third of the way ripe, he sets aside *péah* for the entire field].

הלכה יח
המוכר מקומות מקומות משדהו לאנשים הרבה, אם מכר כל השדה כל אחד ואחד נותן פאה אחת מחלקו שלקח, ואם התחיל בעל השדה לקצור ומכר מקצת ושייר מקצת, בעל השדה נותן פאה הראויה לכל, שכיון שהתחיל לקצור נתחייב בכל, ואם מכר תחלה מפריש הלוקח על מה שלקח ובעל השדה על מה ששייר.

18. In the case of one who sells from different places [a bit from here and a bit from there] in his field to many people, if he [eventually] sold the entire field [this way], each one of the buyers must give *péah* for the lot that they took. But if the

55. A qualification for *péah* is that it is still standing.
56. See Mishnah Péah 3:5.

[original] owner of the field began to harvest it, having sold part and kept part, the owner of the field must give *péah* for the entire field, for when he began to harvest it he became liable for all of it. But if he sold part of it first, the one who takes must set aside [*péah*] from what he took and the owner of the field from what he kept.[57]

הלכה יט

שדה אילן אין מפסיק בה אלא גדר גבוה המבדיל בין האילנות, אבל אם היה הגדר מבדיל מלמטה והבדים והפארות מעורבין מלמעלה ונוגעין בגדר על גבו הרי זה כשדה אחת ונותן פאה לכל.

19. In a field of trees, the only thing that can form a partition is a fence tall enough to separate the trees, but if there is a fence separating the lower part of the trees and the branches and the crowns of the trees are entangled up above, touching one another over the fence, then this counts as one field, and one gives *péah* [in one portion] for it all.[58]

הלכה כ

שנים שלקחו אילן אחד נותנין ממנו פאה אחת, לקח זה צפונו וזה דרומו זה נותן פאה לעצמו וזה נותן פאה לעצמו.

20. Two people who took [produce] from [different branches of] one tree give [together] one portion of *péah*. [But if one] took from the north [of the tree] and the other from the south, then each gives *péah* from his portion separately.[59]

הלכה כא

החרובין כל שאדם עומד בצד חרוב זה וחבירו עומד בצד חרוב זה ורואין זה את זה הרי הן כלן שדה אחת ופאה אחת לכלן, היו שני הצדדין רואין את האמצעיים ואין הצדדים רואין זה את זה מפריש מצד אחד מן הראשונים על האמצעיים ומן האמצעיים על הראשונים, אבל לא יפריש מצד זה על הצד האחר.

21. In the case of carob trees [which grow very tall with a great deal of space in between them], all that someone standing on one side [of the field] with another standing on the other side [of the field] can see counts as one field and one gives one portion of *péah* for them all. If the two sides can see [trees] in between them but they cannot see each other [through the trees], one tithes by dividing the trees in between in proportion to each side, but he may not set aside [*péah*] from one side [of the field] all the way to the other [side, as if it is one large field].[60]

---

57. See Mishnah Péah 3:2. Maimonides' ruling is at variance from the Mishnah.
58. See Mishnah Péah 2:3.
59. See Mishnah Péah 3:5.
60. Referring to Mishnah Péah 2:4, Ravad raises an objection. Whereas Maimonides rules that people must be in sight of one another through the carob trees to form one unit, Ravad claims that it is not the people who must be in sight but the trees themselves. The Mishnah states that carob trees that are all in sight of one another are counted as one unit as far as the giving of

הלכה כב
הזיתים כל מה שיש מהן ברוח אחת מרוחות העיר כגון זיתים שיש במערב העיר כולן או במזרחה הרי הן כשדה אחת ופאה אחת לכלן.

22. In the case of olive trees, all trees located on one side of the city, such as the west of the city or in its entirety, or to the east, count as one field, and one portion of *péah* [is given] for all.

הלכה כג
הבוצר את מקצת כרמו מכאן ומכאן כדי להקל מעל הגפן עד שימצאו שאר האשכולות ריוח ויוסיפו הוא הנקרא מידל, וכבר בארנו שהבוצר מרוח אחת אינו מידל ולפיכך נותן מן הנשאר פאה הראויה לכל, ואף על פי שבצר לשוק, אבל אם הידל למכור בשוק אינו נותן פאה לזה שהידל, הידל להביא בביתו נותן מן הנשאר שהניח לדרוך פאה אחת הראויה לכל.

23. When one harvests grapes partially from different patches of his vineyard in order to lighten the vine so that the remaining space in between the clusters widens, it is called "thinning." We have already explained[61] that one who harvests grapes all from one side is not thinning and therefore must give *péah* for the whole crop, regardless of whether he takes them to market [instead of saving them for wine]. But if he thinned out the vines in order to sell [those grapes] in the market, he does not need to give *péah* for that which he thinned out. But if the grapes that were taken in the thinning out were brought into his home, then he gives *péah* from the remainder that he left to be stamped [in the wine press] as due for the whole crop [including the ones he brought into his house].[62]

---

péah is concerned because of the great height of carob trees. That is, one who climbs up the tree counts the other carob trees that are in sight, regardless of fences in between them, and this constitutes one group of trees. Carob trees, like sycamores, are in a special category because of their height, as seen also in Mishnah Bava Batra 2:11, where it states that one cannot plant a carob tree near a well because of the way it spreads out (presumably with its roots as well as branches).

61. See 2:6.

62. See Mishnah Péah 3:3.

After having explicated the laws of péah, *Maimonides now considers the other categories of "gifts for the poor" one by one, beginning with* leket *("overlooked gleanings"). In trying to define what is considered "overlooked," Maimonides makes clear that stray stalks or sheaves of grain that fall by the wayside during the normal motion of using a scythe fall into this category. Produce for the poor results from the norms of human behavior and not the exceptions. Furthermore, if the owner of the field fails to give the poor their due, he may still make up for it by donating harvested produce but in a costlier fashion.*

הלכה א
איזהו לקט זה הנופל מתוך המגל בשעת קצירה או הנופל מתוך ידו כשמקבץ השבלים ויקצור, והוא שיהיה הנופל שבלת אחת או שתים, אבל אם נפלו שלש כאחד הרי שלשתן לבעל השדה, והנופל מאחר המגל או מאחר היד אפילו שבלת אחת אינה לקט.

1. What is considered *leket*? That which falls from within the scythe at the time of harvesting or that which falls from within one's hand while gathering sheaves that one is about to harvest. And this means one or two stalks that fall, but if three have fallen as one bunch, they belong to the owner of the field. And that which falls after the scythe or from behind the hand, even if it is only one stalk, [is also the owner of the field's] and is not considered to be *leket*.[63]

הלכה ב
היה קוצר ביד בלא מגל הנופל מתוך ידו אינו לקט, אבל התולש דברים התולשים אותם הנופל מתחת ידו לקט, היה קוצר או תולש דבר שדרכו להתלש ואחר שקצר מלא זרועו או תלש מלא קמצו הכהו קוץ ונפל מידו על הארץ הרי זה של בעל הבית.

2. If one is harvesting by hand without a scythe [and it is usual to use a scythe to harvest], that which falls from within the hand is not *leket*, but as for one who picks things [and this is the normal manner to gather them], when they pluck them and something falls from under the hand, then this is *leket*. If one was harvesting or picking something for which it is usual to be plucked by hand and had harvested an armful or had picked a handful and then a thorn stuck him and it fell from his hand to the ground, then this [remains] the household owner's [and does not count as *leket*].[64]

63. See Mishnah Péah 4:10. In other words, any stray stalks that are missed through the normal motion of using a scythe, so long as they do not fall in bunches of three or more and therefore would normally be picked up by the harvester belong to the poor.

64. See Mishnah Péah 4:10.

הלכה ג
היה קוצר ונשארה שבלת אחת שלא נקצרה ונקצר כל שסביבותיה, אם היה ראשה מגיע לקמה שבצדה ויכולה להקצר עם הקמה הרי היא של בעל השדה ואם לאו הרי היא של עניים.

3. If one harvested and there remained one stalk that was not harvested but all around it was harvested, if its end was even with the standing grain that was on the side and it is possible that it will be harvested with the standing grain, then this is the owner of the field's, and if not [that is, it is not close enough to the standing grain to be harvested with it when the reapers come through again,] then this belongs to the poor.[65]

הלכה ד
היו שתי שבולות זו בצד זו, הפנימית יכולה להקצר עם הקמה והחיצונה יכולה להקצר עם הפנימית ואינה יכולה להקצר עם הקמה, הפנימית נצלת ומצלת את החיצונה שהרי היא כנופלת מתוך המגל ואע"פ שעדיין לא נקצרה, והשבלים שבקש הרי הן של בעל השדה.

4. If there were two stalks side by side [next to standing grain], and the one on the inside could be harvested with the standing grain and the outside one could be harvested with the inside one but could not be harvested with the standing grain, the inside one is saved [from being *leket*] and in turn it saves the outside one [from being *leket*],[66] for while it is similar to that which falls within the scythe, nevertheless it still has not been harvested [and therefore it is not *leket*]. And stalks that are covered by the stubble [so that they cannot be seen easily] belong to the owner of the field.[67]

הלכה ה
הרוח שפזרה את העומרים ונתערב קציר של בעל השדה עם הלקט אומדין את השדה כמה לקט היא ראויה לעשות ונותן לעניים מפני שזה אונס, וכמה הוא שיעור זה ארבעה קבין תבואה לכל בית כור.

5. If the wind scatters the sheaves [that are set aside as *leket*], and they became mixed in with the harvested grain that belongs to the owner of the field, they estimate according to the size of the field how much *leket* is appropriate to be provided, and he gives to the poor accordingly because this is a matter of forces beyond his control. How much is the measure [for estimating]? It is four *kavim* of produce for every *bét kor*.[68]

---

65. See Mishnah Péah 5:2. These will be harvested in the normal course of things.
66. See 5:21 and Mishnah Péah 6:8.
67. See 5:3 and Mishnah Péah 5:7.
68. See Mishnah Péah 5:1. In today's terms, according to the calculations found in the tables by Haim Herman Cohn, "Weights and Measures in the Talmud," *Encyclopedia Judaica* 16 (Jerusalem: Keter Publishing Company Ltd., 1972), four *kavim* would equal approximately 3.7 kilograms for every 4.3 acres which would produce about 2,750 kilograms, or only .1%. This is very small. However, in the Jerusalem Talmud Péah 5:1, Rabbi Zeira challenges this measurement and claims that the minimum amount should be four *kavim* for each area that

הלכה ו
לקט שנפל לארץ ולא לקטוהו עניים ובא בעל השדה והגדיש את הקציר שלו על הארץ כיצד הוא עושה, מפנה הגדיש שלו כולו למקום אחר וכל השבלים הנוגעות בארץ כולן לעניים, מפני שאין אנו יודעים אי זו היא מהם שהיתה לקט וספק מתנות עניים לעניים שנאמר תעזוב הנח לפניהם משלך.

6. If *leket* fell to the ground and the poor did not glean them and then the owner of the field came and bundled his harvest from all that was on the ground [including the *leket* left there], what is he supposed to do? He rolls his bundle over entirely to another place, and all the stalks which touch the ground [on the outside of the bundle] are for the poor[69] because it cannot be known which was *leket*, and gifts for the poor that are in doubt are deemed to be for the poor,[70] as it is said, (Lev. 19:10, 23:22) *Leave [them for the poor]*, that which is left before them from your property.

הלכה ז
ולמה אין אומדין אותה וליתן לעניים מה שראויה לעשות לקט, מפני שעבר והגדיש על הלקט קנסוהו, ואפילו היה שוגג ואפילו היה הלקט שעורים והגדיש עליו חטין, ואפילו קרא לעניים ולא באו אפילו הגדישוהו אחרים שלא מדעתו כל הנוגעות בארץ הרי הן לעניים.

7. And why do they not estimate [how much he should give in the preceding situation] and let him give to the poor that which is appropriate to become *leket*? Because he transgressed [the negative *mitzvah* against gathering overlooked gleanings] and bundled the *leket*, [so therefore] they fine him [with this costlier method]. Even if he did so by accident, even if the *leket* were barley and he bundled wheat, even if he called out to the poor and they did not come, and even if others bundled it for him without his knowledge, all that touches the ground is for the poor.

הלכה ח
הצריך לרבץ את שדהו קודם שילקטו העניים לקט שבה אם היזקו מרובה על הפסד הלקט מותר לרבץ, ואם הפסד הלקט מרובה על הפסדו אסור לרבץ, ואם קבץ את כל הלקט והניחו על הגדר עד שיבא העני ויטלנו הרי זה מדת חסידות.

8. If one needs to irrigate his field before the poor glean the *leket* that are in it, if not irrigating would result in more damage [to the owner] than the loss of the *leket* [would do to the poor], then watering is permitted, but if the loss of the *leket*

---

produces a *kor* of grain, which would make more sense. Indeed, there is a dispute in the Jerusalem Talmud about different kinds of measuring and whether or not this leaves enough for the poor. The question that this brings up is whether or not the minimum amounts that one needs to give as gifts for the poor are of significance. Clearly they once were, but their equivalents in today's measurements are ambiguous.

69. This method leaves a much greater quantity for the poor.

70. It is better to err on the side of generosity than on the side of selfishness. See Babylonian Talmud Chullin 134a.

[for the poor] is greater than his loss, then it is forbidden to irrigate.[71] If he [the owner] gathered all the *leket* and laid them against a fence [before he irrigated] so the poor person could come and take them, this is holding oneself to an extreme measure of piety.[72]

הלכה ט
זרעים הנמצאים בחורי הנמלים, אם היו החורים בתוך הקמה הרי הוא של בעל השדה שאין לעניים, מתנה בתוך הקמה, ואם היו במקום שנקצר הרי זה של עניים שמא מן הלקט גררוהו, ואע״פ שנמצא שחור אין אומרים הרי זה משנה שעברה שספק הלקט לקט.

9. As for the seeds that are found in ant holes, if the holes are located within the standing grain, they belong to the owner of the field and not to the poor, for they are placed within the standing grain, but if they are in a place that has been harvested, then these belong to the poor, for perhaps they were buried from *leket*. And even though [a seed] might appear black [from having been there long time], they do not say that it is from the year that has passed [and therefore belongs to the owner], for *leket* that are doubtful are deemed to be *leket* [and are given to the poor].[73]

הלכה י
שבולת של לקט שנתערבה בגדיש הרי זה מפריש שתי שבולות ואומר על אחת מהן אם הלקט היא זו הרי היא לעניים ואם אינה לקט הרי המעשרות)שהיא(שחייבת בהן שבולת זו קבועים בשבולת שנייה, וחוזר ומתנה כן על שבולת שנייה ונותן אחת מהן לעני והאחרת תהיה מעשר.

10. If a stalk of *leket* became mixed with a bundle [for the owner], then he separates two stalks and declares over one of them, "If it is *leket* then it is for the poor and if it is not *leket* then it is for tithes," for the obligation on one of the stalks is connected with the second stalk. He then goes back and gives the second stalk [to the poor], thus giving one of them to the poor and the other for tithing.

הלכה יא
לא ישכור אדם את הפועל על מנת שילקט בנו אחריו, אבל האריסין והחכירין והמוכר קמתו לחבירו לקצור ילקט בנו אחריו, ויש לפועל להביא אשתו ובניו ללקט אחריו, ואפילו שכרו ליטול חצי הקציר או שלישו או רביעו בשכרו.

---

71. See Tosefta Péah 2:21.

72. Maimonides indicates that going to this extent to fulfill the commandment is going above and beyond the necessary requirements and effort. In another place in the *Mishneh Torah*, "Laws on Attributes," 1:4-5, Maimonides considers this level of observance extreme and not necessarily praiseworthy. Whereas the "wise person" lives a balanced life in moderation, the "pious" live life in unnecessary and often dangerous extremities.

73. See Mishnah Péah 4:11. See also the previous law 4:6.

11. A man may not hire a worker on the condition that his [the worker's] son glean after him [and thus guarantee that there will be no *leket*], but one who is betrothed to him [the worker], or a tenant, or if he [the owner] sold his standing grain to his partner to harvest, then his son may glean after him [because these people are in need themselves]. And the worker may bring his wife or his children to glean after him, even if his wages equaled half the value of the harvest or a third or a fourth.[74]

הלכה יב

מי שאינו מניח את העניים ללקט או שהוא מניח אחד ומונע אחד או שמסייע את אחד מהן על חבירו הרי זה גוזל את העניים.

12. One who does not permit the poor to glean or who permits one but prevents another or who assists one of them rather than another is considered a robber of the poor.[75]

הלכה יג

ואסור לאדם להרביץ ארי וכיוצא בו בתוך שדהו כדי שיראו העניים ויברחו, היו שם עניים שאינן ראויין ליטול לקט אם יכול בעל הבית למחות בידן ממחה ואם לאו מניחן מפני דרכי שלום.

13. It is forbidden for a man to let loose a lion or something similar within his field so that the poor see it and flee.[76] If there are poor people who are not supposed to take *leket* [for whatever reason], if the household owner can interfere with what they have taken, he may interfere, but if not, he should leave them be for the sake of peace.[77]

---

74. See Tosefta Péah 3:1 and Mishnah Péah 5:6.

75. See Mishnah Péah 5:6. This law names an important principle, the "robbery of the poor," which is the idea that if one does not give the poor their due then one has essentially stolen from them. The assumption here is that the poor already own the property that is under the owner of the field's supervision, and it is the owner of the field's privilege and duty to transfer the produce to its rightful owners as decreed by God. If one fails in that duty, then one has seized the property of another. There is a "constitutional" relationship that exists between the owner of the field and the poor in relation to God-given, inalienable rights that lay a foundation for their legal responsibilities. However, it is up to human actions to designate and transfer this property before the poor can lay their claim to specific produce. Just as the poor have the constitutional right to certain kinds of produce, so does the owner of a field have a constitutional right to designate and transfer that property. See 2:12-20 for an expansion upon these principles and rights, specifically 2:14 for the rights of the owner of the field.

76. Maimonides implies that the poor must be able to gather their due free from coercion or intimidation.

77. See Babylonian Talmud Bava Metzia 12a. Earlier, in 1:9, the phrase "for the sake of peace" was used in relation to Gentiles, indicating that it was politically expedient to let the poor of Gentiles to gather food alongside the poor of the Jewish community. Here, the "poor people who are not supposed to take *leket*" may be the poor of Gentiles or might be those who are poor but not poor enough to merit public support. In any case, it seems that it would be an

הלכה יד

המפקיר את הלקט עם נפילת רובו אינו הפקר מאחר שנשר רובו אין לו בו רשות.

14. If one [attempts to] declare *leket* as "ownerless" [and thus the community's property] along with the main part of it, which has fallen [to the ground of his crop], then [the *leket*] is not considered "ownerless" because since the main part fell off, it [the *leket*] is no longer his property.[78]

Maimonides changes topics here, moving from one category of "gifts for the poor" to another. Thus far, the paradigm for agricultural produce has been standing grain. Maimonides now looks to another paradigm: the vineyard.

הלכה טו

אי זהו פרט זה גרגר אחד או שני גרגרים הנפרטים מן האשכול בשעת הבצירה, נפלו שלשה גרגרים בבת אחת אינו פרט.

15. What is considered *peret*? These are one or two grapes that have separated from the cluster during the time of the grape harvest. If three grapes fell together as a bunch [at the same time], then this does not count as *peret*.[79]

הלכה טז

היה בוצר וכרת את האשכול והוסבך בעליו ונפל לארץ ונפרט אינו פרט, היה בוצר ומשליך לארץ כשמפנה האשכולות אפילו חצי אשכול הנמצא שם הרי הוא פרט)וכן אשכול שלם שנפרט שם הרי הוא פרט(, והמניח את הכלכלה תחת הגפן בשעה שהוא בוצר הרי זה גוזל את העניים.

16. If one was harvesting grapes and cut down a cluster and it became entangled in the leaves and fell to the ground and [the grapes] fell from the bunch [and became separated], then this is not *peret* [for the intention was that this was one cluster]. [However,] if one was harvesting grapes and threw [the cluster] to the ground and the cluster rolled, or even half a cluster for that matter [obviously not caring for grapes that would separate from the cluster], what [fell away and] could be found counts as *peret*. (So also with a complete cluster that fell away, that this counts as *peret*.) If one places a basket under the vine at the time one is

---

unnecessary hardship on the owner of the field to sort through and assess the needs of the poor, and it is simply easier to let them be.

78. See Mishnah Péah 6:1. In other words, *leket* belongs to the poor, and the owner of the field cannot declare it as "ownerless."

79. See Mishnah Péah 7:3. This parallels the definition of *leket*. One or two grapes indicate stray produce, but three is a significant bunch that the owner would normally pick up. See 4:1.

harvesting grapes [and thereby eliminating any chance for *peret*], then that person is considered a robber of the poor.[80]

Maimonides continues here with a new category of produce, similar to the preceding. Separated grapes, that is, individual grapes that have fallen from the vine, are joined now by malformed grapes, that is, grapes that are unusually small.

הלכה יז
אי זו היא עוללת זה אשכול הקטן שאינו מעובה כאשכול שאין לו כתף, ואין ענביו נוטפות זו על זו אלא מפוזרות, יש לה כתף ואין לה נטף או יש לה נטף ואין לה כתף הרי היא של בעל הכרם, ואם ספק לעניים.

17. What is considered *olélet*? This is a small cluster that is not very dense like a regular cluster and does not have a shoulder[81] and its grapes do not droop down over each other but rather are scattered. If it has a shoulder but no pendant or a pendant but no shoulder, then this belongs to the owner of the vineyard, but if it is in doubt, it belongs to the poor.[82]

הלכה יח
אי זו היא כתף פסיגין המחוברות בשדרה זו על גבי זו, נטף ענבים המחוברות בשדרה ויורדות, והוא שיהיו כל הענבים שבעוללות נוגעין בפס ידו, ולמה נקרא שמו עולל מפני שהוא לשאר האשכולות כעולל לאיש.

18. What is a "shoulder"? Growths which are joined at the stem, one next to the other [forming the wide, upper part of a cluster]. What is a "pendant"? Grapes which are joined to the stem and droop down [forming the lower, cone-shape of the cluster]. In the case of *olélot*, all of the leaves touch within the palm of one's hand.[83] And why is the term [for a malformed grape cluster] *olél* [literally:

80. See Mishnah Péah 7:3. As with previous laws, one should not be overzealous in harvesting but do so in a normal, moderate fashion. That which goes astray is intended by God for the poor.
81. See the next law for an explanation of "shoulder" and "pendant."
82. See Mishnah Péah 7:4.
83. Ravad takes issue with these definitions, citing the Jerusalem Talmud Péah 7:4. There is a dispute between the opinion of Rabbi Yehuda, who gives the definitions that Maimonides puts forward, and an instance cited by Rabbi Chiya who claims that a malformed grape cluster was once weighed and it came out to be an enormous amount. While this cluster was still understood to be malformed, it was clearly much too large to fit into the palm of one's hand. Rather, a third opinion was offered by Rabbi Chinena which said a malformed grape cluster was one where, when it was placed on a table, all of the grapes touched the table's surface. That is, it is not that the entire cluster be of a size as to fit into the palm of one's hand but that it lay flat in an unusual way when one would hold out one's hand horizontally.

infant]? Because it is [small compared] to the rest of the regular clusters the way an infant is to a person.

הלכה יט

ואין בעל הבית חייב לבצור העוללות וליתנן לעניים, אלא הן בוצרין אותן לעצמן וגרגר יחידי הרי היא עוללת.

19. And the owner is not obligated to harvest the *olélot* for the poor, but rather they harvest them for themselves. And a single grape [growing by itself] falls into the category of *olélot.*[84]

הלכה כ

זמורה שהיה בה אשכול ובארכובה של זמורה עוללת אם נקרצה עם האשכול הרי היא של בעל הכרם ואם לאו הרי היא לעניים.

20. In the case of a vine-shoot with a cluster on it that is joined with a vine shoot that has an *olélet* on it, if it [the *olélet*] is clipped with the regular cluster then it belongs to the owner of the vineyard, and if not then it belongs to the poor.

הלכה כא

כרם שכולו עוללות הרי הוא לעניים שנאמר וכרמך לא תעולל אפילו כולו עוללות, ואין הפרט והעוללות נוהגין אלא בכרם בלבד.

21. A vineyard made entirely of *olélot* belongs to the poor, as it is said, (Lev. 19:10) *You shall not pick your vineyard bare [te'olél]* even if it is entirely made of *olélot*. And the categories of *peret* and *olélot* apply only to the vineyard.[85]

הלכה כב

אין העניים זוכין ליקח פרט ועוללות עד שיתחיל בעל הכרם לבצור כרמו שנאמר וכי תבצור כרמך לא תעולל, וכמה יבצור ויהיו זוכין בהן שלשה אשכולות שהן עושין רביע.

22. The poor have no right to take *peret* and *olélot* until the owner of the vineyard begins to harvest his grapes, as it is said, (Deut. 24:21) *When* [and only when] *you pick the grapes of your vineyard, do not go over it again [te'olél].* And how much does he need to harvest until they [the poor] have the right [to start picking]? Three clusters, for this is enough to make a quarter of a *kav*.

הלכה כג

המקדיש כרמו עד שלא נודעו העוללות אין העוללות לעניים, ואם משנודעו העוללות העוללות לעניים ויתנו שכר גידולם להקדש.

23. If one dedicates his vineyard to the Temple before it can become known which will be *olélot*, then the *olélot* do not belong to the poor. But if one waited until *olélot* could be discerned, then they belong to the poor, and they [the poor] dedicate [to the Temple] the increase of their due.[86]

---

84. See Mishnah Péah 7:4.
85. See Mishnah Péah 7:7 where Rabbi Akiba dissents.
86. See Mishnah Péah 7:8.

הלכה כד
הזומר את הגפן אחר שנודעו העוללות הרי זה זומר כדרכו וכשם שכורת האשכולות כך כורת העוללות.

24. One who prunes a vine after it is already known which are *olélot* prunes as usual, and as he cuts the regular clusters, he also cuts the *olélot*.

הלכה כה
נכרי שמכר כרמו לישראל לבצור חייב בעוללות, ישראל ונכרי שהיו שותפים בכרם חלקו של ישראל חייב ושל נכרי פטור.

25. If a Gentile sold his vineyard to a Jew to harvest, then he [the Jew] is obligated to give *olélot*. If a Jew and a Gentile are partners in owning a field, then the Jew owes [*olélot*] from his section and the Gentile is exempt.[87]

הלכה כו
בן לוי שנתנו לו מעשר טבל ומצא בו עוללות נותנן לעני, ואם נקרצת עם האשכול יש לו לעשות תרומת מעשר על מקום אחר.

26. A Levite to whom is given *ma'esar tevel* [produce from which the portion due to the priests, *terumah*, was not separated] and who finds within it *olélot* should give them to the poor. But if it was clipped with regular clusters, then he [the Levite] needs to give *terumat ma'esar* [the portion the Levites must give to the priests] from another crop.[88]

הלכה כז
מי שהיו לו חמש גפנים ובצרם לתוך ביתו, אם לאכול ענבים פטור מן הפרט ומן השכחה ומן הרבעי, וחייב בעוללות, ואם בצרן לעשות יין חייב בכל אלא אם כן שייר מקצתן.

27. In the case of someone who owns five grape vines and brings their produce within his house, if [he harvested them] to eat the grapes, then he is exempt from *peret*, from *shikhecha*, from the fourth year's produce,[89] but owes *olélot*. If he

87. See Tosefta Péah 3:12.

88. Ravad objects and cites Tosefta Péah 3:14, which states that if a Levite is given a portion of grapes in which he finds *olélot*, he need not be concerned that these belong to the poor. As it is explained further in the Jerusalem Talmud Péah 7:4, it is stated that the Levite who finds *olélot* in his portion may declare these as *terumat ma'asér*, that is, the portion the Levites separate from the tithe given to them that they give to the priests, for other produce in another location. Nevertheless, an objection is raised that the Levite is still depriving the poor of their share by designating it as another kind of tithe. Rabbi Avin then comments that the grapes under dispute are not really *olélot* at all but rather the Levite may assume that these malformed grapes were cut as one bunch along with regular grapes and thereby do not belong to the poor. In any case, these sources seem to contradict Maimonides' claim that the Levite should give *olélot* to the poor from their apportioned share.

89. The fourth year of a tree was the first year that one could eat its fruit, and one would offer its fruits to the Temple. See Mishnah Péah 7:6 and Babylonian Talmud Berachot 35a.

harvested them for wine, then he owes everything except if he leaves some of them remaining.[90]

90. Referring to Tosefta Péah 1:10, where the case of one who harvests four or five grape vines and brings them into the house is described, Ravad hastens to include *péah* among the categories from which one is exempt. Ravad also disputes Maimonides last statement, that if the owner of the vines harvested them for wine, then he owes all types of categories unless he left some of them on the vine. Ravad claims that he owes everything even if he leaves some behind, as is stated in the Tosefta.

Maimonides now moves on to agricultural produce that is forgotten, even temporarily, by the owner of the field, and also returns to the paradigm of standing grain. After standing grain is considered, Maimonides addresses other general categories of produce, such as olives. As before, he begins with a technical definition of this kind of produce, the "forgotten," and then explicates ambiguous situations that challenge that definition. Ultimately, the law needs to clarify what kind of behavior demonstrates that something has become forgotten, abandoned, and therefore designated for the poor by God. Mitigating these laws is the human tendency to try to make conditions on farming practices so as to technically "forget" as little as possible. However, as seen explicitly in 5:8, the law of the Torah overrides the owner of the field's self-interested maneuvers.

הלכה א

העומר ששכחוהו פועלים ולא שכחו בעל השדה, שכחו בעל השדה ולא שכחוהו פועלים, שכחוהו אלו ואלו והיו שם אחרים עוברין ורואין אותן בעת ששכחוהו, אינה שכחה עד שישכחוהו כל אדם, ואפילו עומר הטמון אם נשכח הרי זה שכחה.

1. If a sheaf is forgotten by workers but was not forgotten by the owner of the field, or if the owner of the field forgot it but the workers did not forget it, or both of them forgot it but others passed by and saw it at the time that they [the owner and the workers] forgot it, then it does not count as *shikhecha* until everyone forgets it. Even if it is a sheaf that was hidden, if it was forgotten [by everyone], then this is *shikhecha*.[91]

הלכה ב

היה בעל השדה בעיר ואמר יודע אני שהפועלים שכחו עומר שבמקום פלוני ושכחוהו הרי זה שכחה, ואם היה בשדה ואמר כן ושכחוהו אינה שכחה שהשכוח מעיקרו בשדה הוא השכחה, אבל בעיר אפילו זכור ולבסוף שכוח הרי זו שכחה שנאמר ושכחת עומר בשדה ולא בעיר.

2. If the owner of the field was in the city, and he said, "I know that the workers forgot a sheaf in such-and-such a place," and they had in fact forgotten it, then this is *shikhecha.* But if he was in the field and said so and they forgot it, then this is not *shikhecha*, for the act of forgetting is rooted exclusively in the field in order for it to be *shikhecha* [and remembering outside of the domain of the field has no effect]. If one is in the city, even if it is remembered [by someone there] and in the end becomes forgotten [by those in the field], then this is *shikhecha*, as it is said, (Deut. 24:19) *And overlook a sheaf in the field* and not in the city.[92]

---

91. See Mishnah Péah 5:7.

92. See Babylonian Talmud Bava Metzia 11a.

הלכה ג
עמדו העניים בפניו או חיפוהו בקש והוא זוכר את הקש או שהחזיק בו להוליכו לעיר והניחו בשדה ושכחו אינו שכחה, אבל אם נטלו ממקום למקום אע"פ שהניחו סמוך לגפה או לגדיש או לבקר או לכלים ושכחו הרי זה שכחה.

3. If the poor people stood in front of him [the owner, hiding the sheaf], or if it was buried in stubble and he [the owner or the worker] remembered the stubble, or if he took it and brought it to the city and left it in a field [there] and forgot it, then this is not *shikhecha.* But if they took it from place to place [within the field], even if they left it next to a stone wall, a stack, near oxen, or next to tools [which might indicate that it was put there on purpose], and it was forgotten, then this is *shikhecha.*[93]

הלכה ד
נטל עומר להוליכו לעיר והניחו על גבי חבירו ושכח את שניהן, אם זכר העליון קודם שיפגע בו אין התחתון שכחה ואם לאו התחתון שכחה.

4. If he took a sheaf and brought it to the city and placed it on top of another and forgot both of them, if he remembered the top one first and then happened upon it [the bottom one], the bottom one is not *shikhecha,* but if not [that is, if he did not remember the top one], then the bottom one is *shikhecha.*[94]

הלכה ה
עפו עמריו ברוח חזקה לתוך שדה חבירו ושכח שם עומר אינו שכחה שנאמר קצירך בשדך, אבל אם פזר העמרים בתוך שדהו ושכח הרי זו שכחה.

5. If a strong wind blew someone's sheaves into an adjacent field and he [the owner or the worker] forgot the sheaf there, this is not *shikhecha*, for it is said, (Deut. 24:19) *When you reap the harvest in your field* [yours and not anyone

93. See Mishnah Péah 5:7 and Mishnah Péah 6:2. In Mishnah Péah 5:7, we see that it is not *shikhecha* if it was covered up, but it does not mention anything about forgetting. Perhaps the implication is that the poor may have tried to hide it from the owner. Maimonides adopts Hillel's position that the sheaf does qualify as *shikhecha,* rejecting the idea that the poor might have covered it up so as to get more.

94. See Tosefta Péah 3:3 and Babylonian Talmud Sotah 45a. Ravad points out that Maimonides is ruling according to Rabbi Shimon who is stating the dissenting opinion. In the Tosefta, the first opinion is that the top sheaf is not subject to the law of *shikhecha,* presumably because the owner had at one time specifically picked it up to carry it into the city, but the bottom one is. Rabbi Shimon's opinion is that both sheaves are not *shikhecha* in that the top one is linked with the bottom one and in remembering the top one the bottom one is also exempt from being *shikhecha.* In the Jerusalem Talmud Péah 6:3, this idea is expanded upon by Rabbi Zeira who states that it is precisely in remembering the top sheaf that the bottom one is not *shikhecha,* for the top one covers up and hides the bottom sheaf and disqualifies it from being *shikhecha,* just as if it were hidden by clothes or stones (as in the previous law). In this case, the top sheaf is not *shikhecha,* but the bottom one is.

else's], but if it scattered the sheaves within his own field and he forgot [them] then this is *shikhecha.*

הלכה ו

הנוטל עומר ראשון ושני ושלישי ושכח הרביעי, אם היה שם ששי אין הרביעי שכחה עד שיטול החמישי, ואם היו חמשה בלבד משישהא כדי ליטול החמישי הרי הרביעי שכחה.

6. If one takes one sheaf and then a second one and then a third one and forgot the fourth, if there is a sixth one, then the fourth one is not forgotten until he takes the fifth. And if there were only five sheaves, if he waited long enough to take the fifth, then the fourth is *shikhecha.*[95]

הלכה ז

שני עמרים מעורבבין ושכח אחד מהן אינה שכחה עד שיטול את כל סביבותיו.

7. If two sheaves were mixed up, and he forgot one of them, this is not *shikhecha* until he takes all the ones around it.[96]

הלכה ח

הלוף והשום והבצלים וכיוצא בה אע"פ שהן טמונין בארץ יש להן שכחה, הקוצר בלילה ושכח קמה או שעמר בלילה ושכח עומר וכן הסומא ששכח יש להן שכחה, ואם היה הסומא או הקוצר בלילה מתכוין ליטול את הגס אין לו שכחה, וכל האומר הריני קוצר על מנת מה שאני שוכח אני אטול יש לו שכחה שכל המתנה על מה שכתוב בתורה תנאו בטל.

8. Arum, garlic, onions, and similar produce, even though they are buried in the ground, the law of *shikhecha* applies to them. [So also for] the one who harvests at night and forgets standing grain, or one who was binding sheaves at night and forgot a sheaf, and so too with the blind person who forgets [some standing grain or a sheaf], the law of *shikhecha* applies in these situation as well. But if the blind person or the one who harvests at night intends to take only the larger sheaves [and deliberately leave some of the smaller ones behind], then they are not *shikhecha.* But anyone who says, "I am harvesting on the condition that anything I forget I may take [later]," the law of *shikhecha* still applies, for all of the gifts for the poor come from the Torah, and his condition is invalid.[97]

---

95. It has been demonstrated that one sheaf can "save" another, and the question arises here when an observer can decisively say a sheaf has truly been forgotten. If one is taking sheaves, skips two, and goes back and only picks up one of the skipped sheaves, the one left behind is truly forgotten.
96. See Tosefta Péah 3:4.
97. See Mishnah Péah 6:10-11. Human legal stipulations cannot override laws from the Torah.

הלכה ט
תבואה שקצרה עד שלא נגמרה להאכילה לבהמה, וכן אם קצרה אגודות קטנות ולא עשאה עמרים, וכן השומים והבצלים שתלשן אגודות קטנות להמכר לשוק ולא עשאן עמרים להעמיד מהן גורן אין להם שכחה.

9. If grain was harvested before it was finished [ripening] so as to feed cattle, and so also if he harvested them into small bundles and did not make sheaves of them, and so also with garlic and onions that they picked them in small bundles in order to sell them in the market and they did not make sheaves out of them to put them into storage, then the law of *shikhecha* does not apply.[98]

הלכה י
הקוצר שהתחיל לקצור מראש השורה ושכח לפניו ולאחריו, של אחריו שכחה ושלפניו אינו שכחה שנאמר לא תשוב לקחתו אינו שכחה עד שיעבור ממנו ויניחנו לאחריו, זה הכלל כל שהוא בבל תשוב שכחה וכל שאינו בבל תשוב אינו שכחה.

10. If a harvester began to harvest at the beginning of a row and forgot [produce] that was in front of him [that he had not yet gone through] and behind him [that he had gone through], the law of *shikhecha* applies to what was behind him but not to that which is in front of him, as it is said, (Deut. 24:19) *Do not turn back to get it.* It is not *shikhecha* until he has gone through it and left it behind him. A general rule: When "*do not turn back*" applies, so does *shikhecha*, and anything to which "*do not turn back*" does not apply cannot be *shikhecha.*[99]

הלכה יא
שנים שהתחילו לקצור מאמצע השורה זה פניו לצפון וזה פניו לדרום ושכחו לפניהם ולאחריהן, שלפניהם שכחה, מפני שכל אחד מהן זה שלפניו הוא לאחוריו של חבירו, והעומר ששכחוהו לאחוריהן במקום שהתחילו ממנו אינו שכחה, מפני שהוא מעורב עם השורות שמן המזרח למערב והן מוכיחין עליו שאינו שכוח, וכן השורות של עמרים שפינו אותן לגורן והתחילו שנים מאמצע שורה ושכחו עומר באמצע בין אחוריהן אינו שכחה מפני שהוא באמצע השורה שמן מערב למזרח שעדיין לא התחילו בה והיא מוכחת עליו שאינו שכוח.

11. If two people began to harvest from the midst of a row [with some space left in between them] with one facing north and the other facing south, and they forgot [produce] that was before them [that the individual did not get through but which his partner was relying upon him to finish] and after them [that they did not go through because both backs were turned to it right from the start], the law of *shikhecha* applies to that which was before them because what is before one is behind the other [and is *shikhecha* by the other person] but the sheaf which they forgot after them in the place that they started is not *shikhecha* because it is mixed in with the rows [that will be harvested] from east to west which they are

98. See Mishnah Péah 6:10.
99. See Mishnah Péah 6:4.

assuming [will be harvested when people go east and west and that is why they purposefully did not go through it] and thus it is not *shikhecha.* So also with the rows of sheaves which they transfer to storage, for if two begin in the midst of a row and they forget a sheaf that is behind and between them, this is not *shikhecha* because it is in the middle of a row [that also goes] from west to east which they have not begun [to bind] and thus this proves that it is not *shikhecha.*[100]

הלכה יב
הקוצר ואלם אלומות אלומות, ופינה האלומות והן הנקראין עומרים ממקום זה למקום אחר, וממקום השני למקום השלישי, וממקום השלישי לגורן ושכח העומר בשעה שפינה ממקום למקום, אם פינה העומרים למקום שהוא גמר מלאכה ושכחה יש לו שכחה וכשיפנה ממקום שהוא גמר מלאכה לגורן אין לו שכחה, ואם פינה העומרים למקום שאינו גמר מלאכה ושכח אינו שכחה וכשיפנה ממקום שאינו גמר מלאכה לגורן יש לו שכחה.

12. When one is harvesting standing sheaves, one standing sheaf after another, and transfers these sheaves from one place to another, also called *omrim,*[101] from a second place to a third place, and from a third place to the threshing floor storage area, and he forgot a sheaf while transferring it from place to place, if he was transferring sheaves to a place where he had completed the process [of their preparation] and he forgot it, then it is *shikhecha.* If [he forgot it] when he was transferring it from a place where he had completed the process to the threshing floor, then this is not *shikhecha.* And if he was transferring sheaves to a place where he would not complete the process and he forgot one, this is not *shikhecha* [either because he is in the midst of the process]. But if he was transferring from a place where he had not completed the process to the threshing floor, then this is *shikhecha.*[102]

---

100. See Mishnah Péah 6:4. Ravad responds here with an unusually lengthy comment because he apparently feels Maimonides has not explicated the sources completely and properly. First Ravad explains Maimonides' reasoning as he sees it: If someone is gathering sheaves going from north to south, reaches the end of the row and then goes from south to north and so on, if the gatherer passes through and leaves a sheaf behind, Maimonides claims this is *shikhecha.* Ravad claims that Maimonides does not take into account the special circumstances that exist for sheaves left at the ends of rows. The gatherer who goes from north to south could intend to go back and collect some more at the ends of the rows while going east to west. Since the gatherer going east and west is walking perpendicular to his original path, he is not retracing his steps and does not violate the commandment to *not turn back to get it* (Deut. 24:19). This possibility is taught in Tosefta Péah 3:4 and the Jerusalem Talmud Péah 6:3. Thus, what is *shikhecha* at the ends of the rows is not clear until one sees the direction in which one completes the binding of the sheaves. Thus it says in Mishnah Péah 6:3, "In the case of sheaves at the end of rows, whether or not a sheaf is *shikhecha* is proven by the sheaf lying opposite it."

101. The word "sheaf" as it has been translated here has only referred to *omrim.*

102. See Mishnah Péah 5:8.

הלכה יג
אי זהו מקום שהוא גמר מלאכה, זה מקום שדעתו לקבץ כל העומרין שם ולדוש אותן שם או להוליכן שם למקום גדיש שהוא הגורן, ומקום שאינו גמר מלאכה הוא המקום שמקבצין בו העומרים כדי לעשות מהן אלומות גדולות כדי להוליכן למקום אחר.

13. What is a place that is one where he completed the process [of their preparation]? This a place where it is his intention to gather all of the sheaves and from there to thresh them or to bring them to a stack that serves as storage. And a place which is one where he does not complete the process is a place where he has gathered the sheaves in order to make large standing sheaves so that he can bring them to another place.

הלכה יד
שתי כריכות המובדלות זו מזו שכחה, ושלש אינן שכחה, שני עומרים המובדלין זה מזה שכחה, ושלשה אינן שכחה.

14. Two small bundles which can be distinguished one from the other may be *shikhecha*, but three may not count as *shikhecha.* Two sheaves which can be distinguished one from the other may be *shikhecha*, but three may not count as *shikhecha.*[103]

הלכה טו
שני צבורי זיתים וחרובין המובדלין זה מזה שכחה, ושלשה אינם שכחה, שני חוצני פשתן שכחה ושלשה אינם שכחה.

15. Two heaps of olives or carobs that can be distinguished one from the other may be *shikhecha,* but three may not count as *shikhecha.* Two stalks of flax may be *shikhecha,* but three may not count as *shikhecha.*[104]

הלכה טז
שתי גפנים וכן בשאר האילנות שנים המובדלין זה מזה שכחה, ושלשה אינן שכחה שנאמר לעני ולגר תעזוב אותם אפילו היו שנים אחד לעני ואחד לגר.

16. As for two vines, and so also with other trees, two which can be distinguished one from the other may be *shikhecha,* but three may not count as *shikhecha,* as it said, (Lev. 19:10, 23:22) *You shall leave them for the poor and the stranger.* Only if there are two, one for the poor and one for the stranger.[105]

הלכה יז
היו כל העומרים של קב קב ואחד של ארבעה קבין ושכחו הרי זה שכחה, יתר על הארבעה אינו שכחה, וכן אם היו של שני שני קבין ואחד יתר על שמונה קבין אינו שכחה.

---

103. See Mishnah Péah 6:5. Here and in the next three laws, Maimonides upholds the principle that two items of produce go to the poor but three do not. See 4:6.

104. See Mishnah Péah 6:5.

105. See Tosefta Péah 3:5.

17. If [there is a field and] the sheaves are of one *kav* quantity apiece, and then there is one [unusually large sheaf] with four *kavim* quantity and they forget it, then it is *shikhecha.* If it is more than four, then it is not *shikhecha.* So also if [there is a field and] the sheaves are two *kavim* quantity apiece, any sheaf more than eight *kavim* quantity may not be *shikhecha.*[106]

הלכה יח

העומר שיש בו סאתים ושכחו אינו שכחה שנאמר ושכחת עומר בשדה ולא גדיש אע"פ שכולן סאתים סאתים, שכח שני עומרים אע"פ שיש משניהן סאתים הרי אלו שכחה, וכן יראה לי שהן שכחה אפילו היה בשניהן יותר מסאתים.

18. A sheaf that will yield two *seah*[107] and is forgotten does not count as *shikhecha,* as it is said, (Deut. 24:19) *And overlook a sheaf in the field,* and not a stack, even if each sheaf yields two *seah* [and is no different from the others in the field]. If he forgot two sheaves [which between the two add up to two *seah*], even though there is between them two *seah*, this counts as *shikhecha.* So also, it appears to me, that the law of *shikhecha* applies even if they add up to more than two *seah* [such as if each sheaf yielded one and a half *seah* and together made three].[108]

הלכה יט

קמה שיש בה סאתים ושכחה אינה שכחה, אין בה סאתים רואין את השבלים הדקות כאילו הן בריאות וארוכות ואת השדופות כאילו הן מלאוה, ואם היתה ראויה)להיות(הקמה אחר אומדן זה לעשות סאתים ושכחה אינה שכחה.

19. Standing grain that would yield two *seah* which he forgot does not count as *shikhecha.* If it would not yield two *seah*, they view the thin stalks as if they were healthy and long and the blasted ones as if they were full, and if they estimate the standing grain to be fit to yield two *seah* and then he forgot it, this does not count as *shikhecha.*[109]

הלכה כ

שכח סאה תבואה עקורה וסאה שאינה עקורה אינן מצטרפים, ושניהם שכחה, וכן בשום ובבצלים ובפירות האילן אם שכח מקצתן בקרקע ומקצתן תלוש ובשניהם סאתים אינן מצטרפין אלא שניהם שכחה.

20. If he forgot a *seah* of grain that was uprooted and a *seah* of grain that was not uprooted, they do not combine them but rather both of them are *shikhecha.* So also with garlic, onions, and fruits of trees. If he forgot part of them in the ground

106. See Mishnah Péah 6:1.
107. The plural is actually *se'atayim*, indicating a couple or a pair.
108. See Mishnah Péah 6:6.
109. See Mishnah Péah 6:7.

and part of them already picked and combined they make up two *seah*, they do not combine them, but both of them are *shikhecha.*[110]

הלכה כא

השוכח עומר בצד הקמה שאינה שכוחה אינה שכחה, שנאמר כי תקצור ושכחת עומר, עומר שסביבותיו קציר שכחה אבל עומר שסביבותיו קמה אינה שכחה, וכן אם שכח קמה בצד קמה שאינה שכוחה אפילו קלח אחד הרי זו מצלת את השכוחה ויהיה מותר לקחתה, אבל אם שכח עומר או קמה בצד עומר שאינו שכוח אפילו היה בו סאתים אינו מציל אותה והרי השכוח לעניים, אין קמת חבירו מצלת על עומר שלו ואין קמת שעורים מצלת על עומר חטים עד שתהיה הקמה ממין העומר.

21. If one forgets a sheaf next to standing grain that is not forgotten, then this [sheaf] is not *shikhecha*, as it is said, (Deut. 24:19) *When you reap the harvest in your field and overlook a sheaf in the field.* A sheaf in which the area around it is harvested may be *shikhecha,* but a sheaf in which the area around it is standing grain is not *shikhecha.* So also if one forgot standing grain that is next to standing grain that is not forgotten, even one stem [that is not forgotten] saves that which is forgotten and it is permitted to take it, but if he forgot a sheaf or standing grain next to a sheaf that is not forgotten, even if it would yield two *seah*, it does not save it and this is considered *shikhecha* and for the poor.[111] The standing grain of one's fellow does not save his [the original farmer's] sheaf. And the standing grain of barley does not save a sheaf of wheat, that this only applies if the standing grain is of the same type as the [forgotten] sheaf.

הלכה כב

השכוח אילן בין האילנות אפילו היה בו כמה סאין פירות או ששכח שני אילנות הרי הן שכחה, שלשה אינן שכחה.

22. If one forgot a tree that was in the midst of other trees, even if it were to yield several *seah* worth of fruit, or [even] if one forgot two trees, then these are *shikhecha.* Three [trees] may not be *shikhecha.*[112]

הלכה כג

במה דברים אמורים באילן שאינו ידוע ומפורסם במקום כגון שהיה עומד בצד הגת או בצד הפרצה, או במעשיו כגון שהיה עושה זיתים הרבה, או בשמו כגון שהיה לו שם ידוע כגון זית הנטופה בין הזיתים שהוא נוטף שמן הרבה או השפכני או הבישני, אבל אם היה בו אחד משלשה דברים אלו אינו שכחה, שנאמר ושכחת עומר בשדה עומר שאתה שוכחו לעולם ואין אתה יודע בו אלא אם תשוב ותראהו, יצא זה שאתה זוכרו לאחר זמן ואע״פ שלא תפגע בו מפני שהוא ידוע ומפורסם.

23. To what does this refer? To a tree that is not well-known for its place, such as one that stands by a wine vat or by the side of a breach in a wall, or for its productivity, such as one that makes many of olives, or for its name, such as it

110. See Mishnah Péah 6:9.

111. See Mishnah Péah 6:8.

112. See Mishnah Péah 7:1. Ravad disagrees claiming that trees do not fit into this category.

being known as "the olive tree that drips olives" or if it overflows with a great deal of oil or [has a nickname, such as] "the Pourer" or "the Embarrasser" [in that it embarrasses the other trees], or even if it has only one of these three characteristics, the law of *shikhecha* does not apply to it, as it is said, (Deut. 24:19) *Overlook a sheaf in the field*, [which means] a sheaf you have forgotten completely and you would not know it unless you went back and saw it. It is exempt [from the law of *shikhecha*] because one remembers it for a long time, even if [one would only remember that particular produce] by happening upon it, for it is well-known.[113]

הלכה כד

היה מסויים בדעתו הרי זה כמפורסם וידוע, היה עומד בצד הדקל הדקל מסיימו, היו שניהן זית נטופה זה מסיים את זה, היתה כל שדהו זית נטופה ושכח אחת מהן או שתים יש לו שכחה, במה דברים אמורים שלא התחיל באילן זה המפורסם אבל אם התחיל בו ושכח מקצתו הרי זה שכחה, ואף על פי שהוא מפורסם, והוא שיהיה הנשאר בו פחות מסאתים, אבל סאתים אינה שכחה אלא אם כן שכח כל האילן כמו שבארנו.

24. If one had marked it [a certain tree] off in his mind, then this counts as being well-known. If it stood next to a date palm tree, then the date palm tree marks it off. If there are two olive trees that overflow [with oil by their abundant produce], they mark off each other. If an entire field is of olive trees known for overflowing with oil, and he forgot one or two of them, then these are *shikhecha.* To what does this refer? Only when he has not begun [to pick] this well-known tree, but if he began to pick it and forgot part of it, then this does count as *shikhecha*, even if it is well-known. But if what remained was less than two *seah* [then this does not apply]. But if it is of two *seah* then this is not *shikhecha* unless he forgot the whole tree, as was explained.[114]

הלכה כה

זית העומד באמצע השורות לבדו ושלש שורות של זיתים מקיפין אותו משלש רוחותיו אע"פ שאין בכל שורה מהן אלא שני זיתים שכח את האמצעי אינו שכחה, שהרי השורות הסתירוהו, ולמה אמרו זית בלבד מפני שהיה חשוב בארץ ישראל באותו הזמן.

25. An olive tree that stands in the middle of several rows by itself, and three rows of olive trees surround it from three sides, even if each row has only two olive trees, if he forgot the one in the middle, this does not count as *shikhecha,* for the rows [of trees] hid it. Why does this apply to olive trees only? Because they were important in the Land of Israel at that time.[115]

---

113. See Mishnah Péah 7:1.

114. Ravad objects that Mishnah Péah 7:1 does not seem to indicate this.

115. Ravad points out that this view is only according to Rabbi Yosi in Mishnah Péah 7:1. See also Mishnah Péah 7:2.

הלכה כו

איזהו שכחה בעריס, כל שאינו יכול לפשוט את ידו וליטלה, ובכרם משיעבור מן הגפן)או(ומן הגפנים וישכח אותה, בדלית ובדקל משירד הימנו, ושאר כל האילנות משיפנה וילך לו, במה דברים אמורים שלא התחיל בו, אבל אם התחיל בו ושכחו אינה שכחה עד שיבצור את כל סביביו.

26. What is considered *shikhecha* in an arbor? Anything that is beyond one's reach and cannot grasp. In a vineyard? When one has passed by one vine or several vines and forgotten them. In suspended vines or date palm trees? Whatever remains after he has come back down. And as for all the other types of trees? Whatever he leaves behind when he turns and goes. To what situation does this apply? When he has not begun [to harvest the orchard with that tree], but if he began [to harvest the orchard with that tree] and forgot it, it [the first tree] is only *shikhecha* when he has harvested all of the fruit trees from around it [in that orchard].[116]

Maimonides concludes the chapter with a mention of "ownerless property." Another way to abandon property, aside from forgetting it, was to declare it ownerless. In this case, the community appropriates the property, and the owner of the field gives up all benefits and liabilities to that property. The owner cannot, however, declare property ownerless in such a way that he retains the benefits. Either he owns the property, enjoys the produce, and gives the poor their due, or he gives the property to the community and gives up all profit and obligations that ownership entails. Maimonides also makes mention of tithes, transitioning to the topic of the next chapter.

הלכה כז

המפקיר את כרמו והשכים בבקר וזכה בו לעצמו ובצרו חייב בפרט ובעוללות ובשכחה ובפאה שהרי שדך וכרמך אני קורא בו מפני שהיה שלו והרי הוא שלו, אבל אם זכה מן ההפקר בשדה של אחרים הרי זה פטור מן הכל, ובין כך ובין כך פטור מן המעשרות כמו שיתבאר.

27. If one declares one's field "ownerless" [and thus community property] and he [the former owner] then gets up one morning and repossesses it and harvests grapes from it, one is obligated to give *peret*, *olélot*, *shikhecha*, and *péah*, for this is [what is it says in Scripture], (Lev. 19:9-10), *Your field...your vineyard.* I read this to mean that because it was his and now it is his [again], [he is obligated to give these things to the poor]. But if one took possession of that which was declared ownerless from others, then one is exempt from all, and in any case one is exempt from tithes as will be explained.[117]

---

116. See Mishnah Péah 7:2.
117. See Babylonian Talmud Bava Kamma 28a.

With this chapter, Maimonides changes the organization of his exposition. The tithe for the poor, the final form of agricultural produce owed to the poor, fit into a larger system of tithes for the Land of Israel. Maimonides, therefore, explains the entire system of tithes that the rabbis derived from the Torah and places the tithe for the poor in that context.

הלכה א

מתנה אחרת ששית יש לעניים בזרע הארץ והוא המעשר שנותנין לעניים והוא הנקרא מעשר עני.

1. Another, sixth type of gift for the poor from agriculture is the tithe that they give to the poor, and it is called *ma'esar ani* [the "tithe for the poor"].

הלכה ב

וזהו סדר תרומות ומעשרות: אחר שקוצר זרע הארץ או אוסף פרי העץ ותגמר מלאכתו מפריש ממנו אחד מן החמשים, וזהו הנקרא תרומה גדולה ונותנה לכהן, ועל זה נאמר בתורה ראשית דגנך תירושך ויצהרך, ואחר כך מפריש מן השאר אחד מעשרה, וזהו הנקרא מעשר ראשון, ונותנו ללוי, ועל זה נאמר בתורה כי את מעשר בני ישראל וגו׳ ונאמר ולבני לוי הנה נתתי את כל מעשר בישראל.

2. And this is the system of gift-offerings and tithes: After one has harvested the seeds of the earth or gathered the fruit of the trees and has completed one's labor, one must separate out one-fiftieth, and this is called the *terumah gedolah* [the "great gift-offering"], and one gives it to a priest. About this it is said in the Torah, (Deut. 18:4) *You shall also give him the first fruits of your new grain and wine and oil.* Afterwards, one separates from the remainder one-tenth, and this is called *ma'asér rishon* [the "first tithe"], and one gives it to a Levite. About this it is said in the Torah, (Num. 18:24) *For it is the tithes set aside by the Israelites [as a gift to the Eternal hat I give to the Levites as their share]*, and (Num. 18:21) *To the Levites I hereby give all the tithes in Israel.*

הלכה ג

ואחר כך מפריש מן השאר אחד מעשרה והוא הנקרא מעשר שני, והוא לבעליו ואוכלין אותו בירושלים, ועליו נאמר ואם גאל יגאל איש ממעשרו, ועליו נאמר עשר תעשר ואכלת לפני ה׳ אלהיך במקום אשר יבחר.

3. Afterwards, one separates from the remainder one-tenth, and this is called *ma'asér sheni* [the "second tithe"], and this is for the owner to eat in Jerusalem. About this it is said, (Lev. 27:31) *If anyone wishes to redeem any of his tithes, [he must add one-fifth to them]*, and about this it is said, (Deut. 14:22-23) *You shall set aside every tenth year [of all of the yield of your sowing that is brought from the field.] You shall consume the tithes [of your new grain and wine and oil, and the firstlings of your herds and flocks, in the presence of the Eternal your God, in the place where He will choose to establish His name, so that you may learn to revere the Eternal your God forever].*

הלכה ד
על הסדר הזה מפרישין בשנה ראשונה מן השבוע ובשניה וברביעית ובחמישית, אבל בשלישית ובששית מן השבוע אחר שמפרישים מעשר ראשון מפריש מן השאר מעשר אחר ונותנו לעניים והוא הנקרא מעשר עני, ואין בשתי שנים אלו מעשר שני אלא מעשר עני, ועליו נאמר מקצה שלש שנים תוציא את כל מעשר תבואתך בשנה ההיא והנחת בשעריך ובא הלוי, ועליו נאמר כי תכלה לעשר.

4. According to this system, they should tithe, in a seven year cycle, the first, second, fourth, and fifth years, but on the third and the sixth years of the seven year cycle, after one has tithed *ma'asér rishon*, one should take out from the remainder another tithe [one-tenth] and give it to the poor. This is called *ma'esar ani*. In these two years there is no *ma'asér sheni* but instead *ma'esar ani.*[118] About this it is written, (Deut. 14:28-29) *Every third year you shall bring out the full tithe of your yield of that year, but leave it within your settlements. Then the Levite, [who has no hereditary portion as you have, and the stranger, the fatherless, and the widow in your settlements shall come and eat their fill, so that the Eternal your God may bless you in all the enterprises you undertake.]* And about this it is written, (Deut. 26:12) *When you have set aside in full the tenth part [of your yield in the third year--the year of the tithe--and have given it to the Levite, the stranger, the fatherless, and the widow, that they may eat their fill in your settlements].*

הלכה ה
שנת השמטה כולה הפקר ואין בה לא תרומה ולא מעשרות כלל לא ראשון ולא שני ולא מעשר עני, ובחוצה לארץ שאין בה שמטת קרקע מפרישין בארץ מצרים ובעמון ובמואב מעשר ראשון ומעשר עני, מפני שהארצות אלו קרובות לארץ ישראל כדי שיהיו עניי ישראל נסמכין עליה בשביעית, והלכה למשה מסיני שיהיו מפרישים בארץ עמון ומואב מעשר עני בשביעית, אבל בארץ שנער מפרישין בשביעית מעשר שני כסדר רוב השנים.

5. In the Sabbatical year, everything is considered "ownerless" [and thus community property] and there are no gift-offerings or tithes at all, not *ma'aser rishon*, not *ma'asér sheni*, not *ma'esar ani*, and outside of the Land of Israel there is no sabbatical for the land. [However,] they tithe in Egypt, Amon, and Moav *ma'asér rishon* and *ma'esar ani* because these lands are close to the Land of Israel so that the poor of Israel may be sustained on it during the seventh year. This is the law of Moses at Sinai[119] that they tithe in the lands of Amon and Moav *ma'esar ani* in the seventh year, but in Shinar they separate out *ma'aser sheni* in the seventh year according to the system of the majority of the years.[120]

118. See Babylonian Talmud Rosh Hashanah 12b.
119. See 3:15.
120. See Mishnah Yada'yim 4:3.

הלכה ו
מעשר ראשון שלקח הלוי מפריש ממנו אחד מעשרה ונותנו לכהן והוא הנקרא תרומת מעשר, ועליו נאמר ואל הלוים תדבר.

6. As for *ma'asér rishon* that was taken for the Levite, he [the Levite] separates from it one-tenth and gives it to a priest. It is called *terumat ma'aser* [the "gift offering of the tithe"], and about this it is written, (Num. 18:26) *Speak to the Levites [and say to them: When you receive from the Israelites their tithes, which I have assigned to you as your share, you shall set aside from them one-tenth of the tithe as a gift to the Eternal].*

הלכה ז
בעל השדה שעברו עליו עניים והיה לו שם מעשר עני, נותן לכל עני שיעבור עליו מן המעשר כדי שבעו שנאמר ואכלו בשעריך ושבעו.

7. When the poor pass by an owner of a field, and he has *ma'esar ani*, he gives to each poor person who comes before him his fill from the tithe, as it is said, (Deut. 14:29) *In your settlements shall come and eat their fill.*

הלכה ח
כדי שבעו כמה אם מן החטים נותן לא יפחות מחצי קב, ואם מן השעורים לא יפחות מקב, ואם מן הכוסמין לא יפחות מקב, ומן הגרוגרות לא יפחות מקב, ואם מן הדבלה לא יפחות ממשקל חמש ועשרים סלע, ואם מן היין לא יפחות מחצי לוג, ואם מן השמן לא יפחות מרביעית, ואם מן האורז רובע הקב, נתן לו ירק נותן לו משקל ליטרא והוא משקל חמשה ושלשים דינר, מן החרובין שלשה קבין, מן האגוזים עשרה, מן האפרסקין חמשה, מן הרמונים שנים, אתרוג אחד, ואם נתן לו משאר הפירות לא יפחות מכדי שימכרם ויקח בדמיהן מזון שתי סעודות.

8. How much is (Deut. 14:29) *their fill*? If it is from wheat, one should not give less than a half a *kav*. If it is from barley, not less then one *kav*. If it is from spelt, not less than one *kav*. If it is from dried figs, not less than one *kav*. And if it is from fig cakes, not less than one *shekel* and five hundred twenty *selah*. If from wine, not less than half a *log*. If from oil, not less than one-fourth a *kav*. And if from rice, not less then one-fourth of a *kav*. If he gives from green herbs, he gives him a *shekel* of a *litre* when a *shekel* is thirty-five *dinarim*. From carobs, three *kavim*. From nuts, ten. From peaches, five. From pomegranates, two. [From] citrons, one. And if he gave from the remainder of fruits, [he gives him] not less than enough for him to sell in the market and take from their value food for two meals.[121]

121. See Mishnah Péah 8:5.

הלכה ט
היה לו דבר מועט והעניים מרובין ואין בו כדי ליתן לכל אחד ואחד כשיעור נותן לפניהם והן מחלקין ביניהם.

9. If he only had a small amount of food and there a great many poor people so that he cannot give to each and every one according to the right measure, he gives [the whole] to them, and they divide it up amongst themselves.[122]

הלכה י
ומעשר עני המתחלק בגורן אין בו טובת הנאה לבעלים אלא העניים באים ונוטלין על כרחו ואפילו עני שבישראל מוציאין אותו מידו, אבל המתחלק בבית יש לו טובת הנאה לבעלים ונותנו לכל עני שירצה.

10. If *ma'esar ani* is divided from the store-chamber, the owners have no right to decide how it is to be apportioned among the poor. Only the poor may come and take regardless of the owner's feelings on the matter. And even if [the owner] is [also] a poor person of Israel, they take it [the tithe] from his possession [for distribution]. But if they divide it up in [his] home [instead of at the store-chamber], then the owner has the right to give it to the poor person that he wants.[123]

הלכה יא
היה לו מעשר בגורן ורצה ליתנו לעני קרובו או מיודעו, יש להפריש מחצה ליתנו לו, והחצי מחלקו לכל עני שיעבור כשיעור שאמרנו.

11. If he had the tithe in the store-chamber, and he wanted to give it to a certain poor relative or someone known to him, he may separate out up to half of it to give to him, and the other half is divided among all the poor who come with the method described previously.[124]

הלכה יב
במה דברים אמורים שאינו נותן לעני אלא כדי שבעו בשדה, אבל אם היה המעשר בבית מחלקו לכל העניים אפילו כזית כזית, שאינו מצווה ליתן כדי שבעו אלא בשדה, שהרי אינו מוצא שם ליקח שנאמר ואכלו בשעריך ושבעו.

12. When does it apply that one gives to the poor in order to give them their fill? When it is from the field, but if he had the tithe in his home [because he was poor himself], they divide it among all the poor people, even if it is only a little bit for each, for one is only commanded to give to satisfy his [the poor person's] fill only from the field, for one finds that this is the case in the verse, (Deut. 14:29) *In your settlements shall come and eat their fill.*

---

122. See Mishnah Péah 8:6.
123. See Babylonian Talmud Nedarim 84b and Chullin 131a.
124. See Mishnah Péah 8:6.

הלכה יג
באו איש ואשה לבית, נותנין לאשה תחלה ופוטרין אותה ואחר כך נותנין לאיש, אב ובנו, איש וקרובו, שני אחין, שני שותפין, שהיה אחד מהן עני נותן לו האחר מעשר עני שלו.

13. If a man and a woman come [begging] to a house, they should give to the woman first and then send her away and then afterwards give to the man. [In the cases of] a father and his son, a man and his relative, two brothers, two partners, when one of them becomes poor, the other one gives *ma'esar ani* to him.[125]

הלכה יד
שתי עניים שקבלו שדה באריסות, זה מפריש מעשר עני מחלקו ונותנו לחבירו, וכן חבירו מפריש מחלקו ונותן לו.

14. If there are two poor people who rented a field in partnership [with the owner], one may separate out *ma'esar ani* and give it to the other [his partner], and so may the other take out from his share and give it to him.[126]

הלכה טו
המקבל שדה לקצור אסור בלקט שכחה ופאה ומעשר עני, אימתי בזמן שקבלה ממנו ליקח חלק בכל השדה כגון שנתן לו שלישה או רביעה בשכרו, אבל אם אמר לו בעל השדה שליש מה שאתה קוצר בלבד הוא שלך או רביע מה שתקצור הרי זה אין לו כלום עד שיקצור, ובשעת הקציר הוא עני, לפיכך מותר בלקט שכחה ופאה, ואסור במעשר עני שאין מפרישין מעשר עני אלא אחר שקצר והרי זכה בחלקו שקצר.

15. If one [poor person] receives a field to harvest, it is forbidden [for him] to take out [in addition to the produce of the field itself] *leket*, *shikhecha*, *péah*, and *ma'esar ani* [for his own benefit]. When is this? [In the situation where] he receives it and can take part of the whole field's harvest, such as when one gives him a third or a fourth as his wages. But if the owner of the field said to him, "What you can harvest yourself from this one-third is yours," or "What you will harvest from this fourth," then he has nothing until he has harvested it. While he is harvesting, therefore, he is poor, and therefore he may take *leket*, *shikhecha*, and *péah* [for himself], but he is forbidden to take *ma'esar ani* because they only separate out *ma'esar ani* after it is all harvested and he has at that point taken possession of his portion that he harvested [and is no longer poor].[127]

הלכה טז
המוכר את שדהו קרקע ופירות והעני, הרי זה מותר בלקט שכחה ופאה ומעשר עני שלה, והלוקח אסור בהן אע״פ שעדיין לא נתן דמים, ואפילו לוה הדמים ולקחה הרי זה אסור במתנות עניים.

16. If one sells his field, including the land and the produce, and then he becomes poor, he is permitted to take its [the land's] *leket*, *shikhecha*, *péah*, and *ma'esar*

125. See Babylonian Talmud Yevamot 100a and Kiddushin 32a.
126. See Mishnah Péah 5:5.
127. See Mishnah Péah 5:5.

ani. But the purchaser is forbidden to take them [these gifts if he is poor].[128] Even if he [the purchaser] has not yet been paid and even if he borrowed money [for the purchase], he is still forbidden to take the gifts for the poor.

הלכה יז

מעשר עני אין פורעין ממנו מלוה, ואין משלמין ממנו את התגמולין, אבל משלמין ממנו דבר של גמילות חסדים וצריך להודיעו שהוא מעשר עני, ואין פודין בו שבויים, ואין עושין בו שושבינות, ואין נותנין ממנו דבר לצדקה, ונותנין אותו לחבר עיר בטובת הנאה, ואין מוציאין אותו מהארץ לחוץ לארץ שנאמר והנחת בשעריך ונאמר ואכלו בשעריך ושבעו.

17. One may not use *ma'esar ani* to repay a loan, and one may not pay back a favor from it [*ma'esar ani*], but they may pay out of it something for an act of loving kindness so long as he informs him that it comes from *ma'esar ani.* But they may not use it to redeem captives [by paying their ransom from *ma'esar ani*], or buy wedding gifts, or give *tzedakah*, but they may give it to a town scholar for his benefit.[129] They may not, however, take it from the Land of Israel to outside the Land of Israel, as it is said, (Deut. 14:28) *But leave it within your settlements*, and it is said, (Deut. 26:12) *That they may eat their fill in your settlements* [teaching that it must be used within the Land of Israel].

128. See Mishnah Péah 5:6.
129. See Tosefta Péah 4:16.

The beginning of this chapter marks a major turning point of the treatise. Having explained the agricultural laws of "gifts for the poor," Maimonides now moves explicitly onto tzedakah, *material giving in righteousness to the poor, immediately applicable in an urban situation. Giving to the poor now primarily takes the form of giving money or collecting coins from people on the street. Maimonides thus spends the rest of the treatise on the last two commandments of his introductory list, not to harden one's heart against the poor and to give generously. Maimonides highlights the psychological aspects of giving to the poor, prescribing actions in case one encounters resistance due to pride. Mitigating circumstances are also present in collecting* tzedakah, *in that even poor people are required to give but not so that they increase their hardship. In this chapter, Maimonides wrestles with the issues of how much to give, from whom and to whom.*

הלכה א

מצות עשה ליתן צדקה לעניים כפי מה שראוי לעני, אם היתה יד הנותן משגת, שנאמר פתוח תפתח את ידך לו ונאמר והחזקת בו גר ותושב וחי עמך ונאמר וחי אחיך עמך.

1. It is a positive *mitzvah* to give *tzedakah* to the poor according to what is fitting for the poor person if he has the means to do so, as it is said, (Deut. 15:8) *Rather, you must open your hand and lend him sufficient for whatever he needs.* And it is said, (Lev. 25:35) *[If your kinsman, being in straits, comes under your authority,] and you hold him as though a resident alien, [let him live by your side:]* And it is said (Lev. 25:36), *[Do not exact from him advance or accrued interest, but fear your God.] Let him live by your side as your kinsman.*[130]

הלכה ב

וכל הרואה עני מבקש והעלים עיניו ממנו ולא נתן לו צדקה עבר בלא תעשה שנאמר לא תאמץ את לבבך ולא תקפוץ את ידך מאחיך האביון.

2. Anyone who sees a poor person begging and averts his eyes from him and does not give him *tzedakah* transgresses a negative *mitzvah*, as it is said, (Deut. 15:7) *[If, however, there is a needy person among you, one of your kinsmen in any of your settlements in the land that the Eternal your God is giving you,] do not harden your heart and shut your hand against your needy kinsman.*

הלכה ג

לפי מה שחסר העני אתה מצווה ליתן לו, אם אין לו כסות מכסים אותו, אם אין לו כלי בית קונין לו, אם אין לו אשה משיאין אותו, ואם היתה אשה משיאין אותה לאיש, אפילו היה דרכו של זה העני

130. See Babylonian Talmud Ketubot 67b-68a.

לרכוב על הסוס ועבד רץ לפניו והעני וירד מנכסיו קונין לו סוס לרכוב עליו ועבד לרוץ לפניו שנאמר די מחסורו אשר יחסר לו, ומצווה אתה להשלים חסרונו ואין אתה מצווה לעשרו.

3. One is commanded to give to a poor person according to what he lacks. If he has no clothes, they clothe him. If he has no utensils for a house, they buy [them] for him. If he does not have a wife, they arrange a marriage for him. If [the poor person] is a woman, they arrange a husband for marriage for her. Even if it was the custom of [a person who was rich but is now] a poor person to ride on a horse with a servant running in front of him, and this is a person who fell from his station, they buy him a horse to ride upon and a servant to run in front of him, as it is said, (Deut. 15:8) *Sufficient for whatever he needs.* You are commanded to fill whatever he lacks, but you are not commanded to make him wealthy.[131]

הלכה ד

יתום שבא להשיאו אשה, שוכרין לו בית ומציעים לו מטה וכל כלי תשמישו ואחר כך משיאין לו אשה.

4. In the case of an orphan who wants to marry a woman [and lacks the means to do so], [first] they pay for a house for him and arrange for a bed for him and all that he needs for the household, and afterwards they arrange a marriage for him.

הלכה ה

בא העני ושאל די מחסורו ואין יד הנותן משגת נותן לו כפי השגת ידו וכמה עד חמישית נכסיו מצוה מן המובחר, ואחד מעשרה בנכסיו בינוני, פחות מכאן עין רעה, ולעולם לא ימנע עצמו משלישית השקל בשנה, וכל הנותן פחות מזה לא קיים מצוה, ואפילו עני המתפרנס מן הצדקה חייב ליתן צדקה לאחר.

5. If a poor person comes and asks for what is sufficient to fill his needs and one does not have the means to provide it for him, one gives according to his means. How much is this? One-fifth of one's assets is the best possible way, but one-tenth is the usual way. Less than this is a bad sign, and never should one restrain himself from a third of a *shekel* a year. Anyone who has not given at least this much has not fulfilled the *mitzvah*.[132] Even a poor person who lives on *tzedakah* is obligated to give *tzedakah* to another.[133]

הלכה ו

עני שאין מכירין אותו ואמר רעב אני האכילוני אין בודקין אחריו שמא רמאי הוא אלא מפרנסין אותו מיד, היה ערום ואמר כסוני בודקין אחריו שמא רמאי הוא, ואם היו מכירין אותו מכסין אותו לפי כבודו מיד ואין בודקין אחריו.

6. If a poor person who is unknown [in the area] has said, "I am hungry; please feed me," They do not check into his background lest he be an impostor, but rather they feed him immediately. If he was naked and said, "Clothe me," they do

131. See Babylonian Talmud Ketubot 67b.
132. See Babylonian Talmud Bava Batra 9a.
133. See Babylonian Talmud Gittin 7b.

check on his background lest he be an impostor, but if they know him, they clothe him according to his honor immediately and they do not check on him.[134]

הלכה ז

מפרנסין ומכסין עניי עכו"ם עם עניי ישראל מפני דרכי שלום, ועני המחזר על הפתחים אין נזקקין לו למתנה מרובה אבל נותנין לו מתנה מועטת, ואסור להחזיר את העני ששאל ריקם ואפילו אתה נותן לו גרוגרת אחת שנאמר אל ישוב דך נכלם.

7. They provide for and clothe the poor of Gentiles along with the poor of Israel for the sake of peaceful relations.[135] And if there is a poor person who goes door to door, they are not obligated to give him a large gift, but rather they give him a small gift. It is forbidden to turn away a poor person who asks empty handed, even if you give him a single dry fig, as it is said, (Psalms 74:21) *Let not the downtrodden be turned away disappointed; [let the poor and needy praise Your name]*.

הלכה ח

אין פוחתין לעני העובר ממקום למקום מככר אחד הנמכר בפונדיון כשהיו החטים ארבע סאין בסלע וכבר בארנו כל המדות, ואם לן נותנין לו מצע לישן עליו וכסת ליתן תחת מראשותיו, ושמן וקטנית, ואם שבת נותנין לו מזון שלש סעודות ושמן וקטנית ודג וירק, ואם היו מכירין אותו נותנין לו לפי כבודו.

8. They may not give to a poor person who goes from place to place less than a loaf of bread which when sold is worth a dupondium when wheat is worth four *se'in* for a *selah,* and we have already explained the ways [this is done]. And if he stays overnight, they give him a blanket with which to sleep and a cushion to put under his head, some oil and some beans, and if it is the Sabbath, they give him enough food for three meals and oil, beans, fish, and green herbs. If they know him, they give to him according to his honor.[136]

הלכה ט

עני שאינו רוצה ליקח צדקה מערימין עליו ונותנין לו לשם מתנה או לשם הלואה, ועשיר המרעיב את עצמו ועינו צרה בממונו שלא יאכל ממנו ולא ישתה אין משגיחין בו.

9. If a poor person does not want to take *tzedakah*, they deal subtlety with him and give to him in the name of a gift or a loan, but as for a wealthy person who makes himself go hungry and looks with sorrow on his wealth and will not eat or drink, they do not pay attention to him.[137]

---

134. See Babylonian Talmud Bava Batra 9a, the opinion of Rabbi Yehudah.
135. See Babylonian Talmud Gittin 61a and Bava Batra 9a.
136. See Mishnah Péah 8:7.
137. See Babylonian Talmud Ketubot 67b.

הלכה י
מי שאינו רוצה ליתן צדקה או שיתן מעט ממה שראוי לו, בית דין כופין אותו ומכין אותו מכת מרדות עד שיתן מה שאמדוהו ליתן, ויורדין לנכסיו בפניו ולוקחין ממנו מה שראוי לו ליתן, וממשכנין על הצדקה ואפילו בערבי שבתות.

10. In the case of one who does not want to give *tzedakah* or who gives less than he should, a court should beat him with blows of chastisement until he gives what they estimate he should. They should bring down his money in front of his face and take from him what he should have given, and they may pawn his property for *tzedakah*, even if it is on the eve of the Sabbath.[138]

הלכה יא
אדם שוע שהוא נותן צדקה יותר מן הראוי לו, או שמיצר לעצמו ונותן לגבאים כדי שלא יתבייש אסור לתובעו ולגבות ממנו צדקה, וגבאי שמכלימו ושואל ממנו עתיד להפרע ממנו שנאמר ופקדתי על כל לוחציו.

11. If a man who is in hardship who gives *tzedakah* more than he should, or who afflicts himself and gives to the collectors so as not to be embarrassed, it is forbidden to make a claim of him or collect *tzedakah* from him. The collector who shames him and asks [for *tzedakah*] from him in the future will be punished, as it is said, (Jeremiah 30:20) *I will deal with all his oppressors.*[139]

הלכה יב
אין פוסקין צדקה על יתומים ואפילו לפדיון שבויים ואע"פ שיש להם ממון הרבה, ואם פסק הדיין עליהם כדי לשום להן שם מותר, גבאי צדקה לוקחין מן הנשים ומן העבדים ומן התינוקות דבר מועט, אבל לא דבר מרובה, שחזקת המרובה גנבה או גזל משל אחרים, וכמה הוא מועט שלהן הכל לפי עושר הבעלים ועניותן.

12. They do not take *tzedakah* from orphans, even for the ransom of captives, even if they have a great deal of money, but a judge may decree such for them for the sake of their reputation. Collectors of *tzedakah* may take a small amount from women, servants, and children, but they may not take a large amount, [for a large amount may have been the result of] thievery and robbery from others. And what is the smallest amount they may give? All is according to the wealth of their masters and their poverty.[140]

הלכה יג
עני שהוא קרובו קודם לכל אדם, עניי ביתו קודמין לעניי עירו, עניי עירו קודמין לעניי עיר אחרת שנאמר לאחיך לענייך ולאביונך בארצך.

13. A poor person who is a relative takes precedence over anyone else. The poor of one's household take precedence over the poor of one's city. The poor of one's

138. See Babylonian Talmud Ketubot 49b and Bava Batra 8b.
139. For example, see Babylonian Talmud Bava Batra 8b, Shabbat 156b and the Introduction.
140. See Babylonian Talmud Bava Batra 8b.

city take precedence over the poor of another city, as it is said, (Deut. 15:11) *Open your hand to the poor and needy kinsman in your land.*[141] A new principle becomes present here. As opposed to giving agricultural produce, which was on a strict "first-come, first-serve" basis, family and community relationships now dictate the giving of *tzedakah*.

הלכה יד

מי שהלך בסחורה ופסקו עליו אנשי העיר שהלך שם צדקה הרי זה נותן לעניי אותה העיר, ואם היו רבים ופסקו עליהן צדקה נותנין וכשבאין מביאין אותה עמהן ומפרנסין בה עניי עירם, ואם יש שם חבר עיר יתנוה לחבר עיר והוא מחלקה כמו שיראה לו.

14. If one engages in trade [and travels between cities] and the authorities of a city exact *tzedakah* from him when he traveled through [for the needs of the city], then this [money] should be given to the poor of that city. But if there are many [such traders], and the authorities of the city exact *tzedakah* from them when they come through, then [they pay it in that city, but] they bring it back with them and give it to the poor of their city [of origin].[142] But if there is a special town scholar, he distributes the *tzedakah* as he sees fit.

הלכה טו

האומר תנו מאתים דינר לבית הכנסת או תנו ספר תורה לבית הכנסת יתנו לבית הכנסת שהוא רגיל בו, ואם היה רגיל בשנים יתנו לשניהן, האומר תנו מאתים דינרין לעניים יתנו לעניי אותה העיר.

15. One who says, "Give 200 *dinarin* for the synagogue" or, "Donate a Torah scroll to the synagogue," they should give to the synagogue which he usually attends. And if he usually attends two [synagogues], then he should give to both of them. If one says, "Give 200 *dinarin* to the poor," they should give to the poor of that city.[143]

---

141. See Babylonian Talmud Bava Metzia 71a.
142. See Babylonian Talmud Megillah 27a.
143. See Tosefta Bava Kama 11:3.

This chapter deviates from the main topic of tzedakah *and covers three closely related topics: pledges, donations, and the redemption of captives. The section on pledges deals with the laws of vows and what is considered binding and what is not. The main principle is that if one has made a pledge to charity, one should fulfill it as quickly as possible, not only because of the need for* tzedakah *but because one does not want to become liable for breaking a pledge. The topic of donations also brings up relations to the Gentile community once more, and the laws on the freeing of captives held for ransom, a situation that involved the collection of money, reveal a harsh reality in the history of the Jewish people.*

הלכה א

הצדקה הרי היא בכלל הנדרים, לפיכך האומר הרי עלי סלע לצדקה, או הרי סלע זו צדקה חייב ליתנה לעניים מיד ואם איחר עבר בבל תאחר שהרי בידו ליתן מיד ועניים מצויין הן, אין שם עניים מפריש ומניח עד שימצא עניים, ואם התנה שלא יתן עד שימצא עני אינו צריך להפריש, וכן אם התנה בשעה שנדר בצדקה או התנדב אותו שיהיו הגבאין רשאין לשנותה ולצורפה בזהב הרי אלו מותרין.

1. A [pledge to] *tzedakah* is a form of a vow, and therefore one who says, "I pledge to give a *selah* for *tzedakah*," or "This *selah* is for *tzedakah*" is obligated to give it to the poor immediately,[144] and if he delays, then he has transgressed the commandment not to delay [fulfilling a vow] (Deut. 23:22). Thus, if poor people can be found there [when he makes the vow], he should give it [to them] immediately. If there are no poor people there, he should set it aside and leave it until he happens upon some poor people. But if he stipulates that he will not give [the coin] until he encounters a poor person, then he need not set it aside. So also if he makes the condition at the time he took the vow for *tzedakah* or to donate something that the collectors are permitted to exchange it or to change it with a goldsmith, then they are permitted to do so.

הלכה ב

המתפיס בצדקה חייב כשאר הנדרים, כיצד אמר הרי סלע זו כזו הרי זו צדקה, המפריש סלע ואמר הרי זו צדקה ולקח סלע שנייה ואמר וזו הרי שנייה צדקה, ואע"פ שלא פירש.

2. One who connects pledges of *tzedakah* is as obligated with one vow as with another. How so? [This applies] if he said, "This *selah* is like that *selah*, then that one is for *tzedakah*." If he sets aside a *selah* and said, "This is for *tzedakah*," and then he took out a second *selah* and said, "And this second one is for *tzedakah*" even though he did not set it aside from the start.[145]

144. See Babylonian Talmud Rosh Hashanah 6a.
145. See Babylonian Talmud Nedarim 7a.

הלכה ג

הנודר צדקה ולא ידע כמה נדר יתן עד שיאמר לא לכך נתכוונתי.

3. One who took a vow for *tzedakah* without knowing how much he vowed should give until he says, "This is not what I intended."[146]

הלכה ד

אחד האומר סלע זו צדקה או האומר הרי עלי סלע לצדקה והפרישו, אם רצה לשנותו באחר מותר, ואם משהגיע ליד הגבאי אסור לשנותו, ואם רצו הגבאים לצרף המעות ולעשותן דינרין אינן רשאין אלא אם אין שם עניים לחלק מצרפין לאחרים, אבל לא לעצמן.

4. If one says, "This *selah* is for *tzedakah*," or one who says, "I owe a *selah* for *tzedakah*," and sets one aside, if he wants to, he may exchange it [that particular coin] for another, but if it has reached the hand of the collector, it is forbidden to exchange it. If the collectors want to combine the small coins for *dinarin* [which are of larger value], they are only permitted to do so if there are no poor people around to whom they need to distribute it. They may combine the coins [for coins of larger value] for the sake of others, but not for themselves.[147]

הלכה ה

היה לעניים הנאה בעיכוב המעות ביד הגבאי כדי לעשות לאחרים ליתן, הרי אותו הגבאי מותר ללוות אותם המעות של עניים ופורע שהצדקה אינה כהקדש שאסור ליהנות בו.

5. If the poor would benefit from keeping the coins in the possession of the collector so that they would thereby make others give [because they would see money in the box and feel compelled to give as others have done], then that collector is permitted to borrow the coins of the poor and make payments [with them], for *tzedakah* is not like sanctified property from which it is forbidden to derive any benefit.[148]

Maimonides moves from the topic of pledges to the topic of donations. He may do so because he is explaining topics brought up in the Babylonian Talmud Arakhin 6a-b for laws 4-8. Even donations to the Temple in Jerusalem, in relation to the Gentile community, are considered here. One can see the disparity of power between the Jewish community and the ruling Gentile authority. Numerous times in history, Jewish experience taught that dependence upon Gentile authorities ought to be minimized.

---

146. See Mishnah Menachot 13:4.
147. See Babylonian Talmud Arachin 6a.
148. See Babylonian Talmud Arakhin 6b.

הלכה ו
מי שהתנדב מנורה או נר לבית הכנסת אסור לשנותה, ואם לדבר מצוה מותר לשנותה, אע"פ שלא נשתקע שם בעליה מעליה אלא אומרים זו המנורה או נר של פלוני, ואם נשתקע שם הבעלים מעליה מותר לשנותה אפילו לדבר הרשות.

6. If someone who donates a menorah or a lamp to a synagogue, it is forbidden to exchange it, but if it is for the sake of a *mitzvah,* it is permitted to exchange it even though the name of the donor has not become lost and people can say, "That menorah" or "That light is from so-and-so." And if the name of the donor became lost [with all the other goods and donations], then it is even possible to exchange it for a secular matter [as opposed to a *mitzvah*].[149]

הלכה ז
במה דברים אמורים בשהיה המתנדב ישראל, אבל אם היה עכו"ם אסור לשנותה אפילו לדבר מצוה עד שישתקע שם בעליה מעליה, שמא יאמר העכו"ם הקדשתי דבר לבית הכנסת של יהודים ומכרוהו לעצמן.

7. To what does this refer? To a situation when a Jew makes the donation, but if a Gentile makes a donation, it is forbidden to exchange it, even for the sake of a *mitzvah,* until the donor's identity has become lost, lest the Gentile say, "I consecrated something to the synagogue of the Jews, and they sold it for themselves."[150]

הלכה ח
עכו"ם שהתנדב לבדק הבית אין מקבלין ממנו לכתחלה, ואם לקחו ממנו אין מחזירין לו, היה הדבר מסויים כגון קורה או אבן מחזירין לו כדי שלא יהא להן דבר מסויים במקדש שנאמר לא לכם ולנו וגו', אבל לבית הכנסת מקבלין מהן לכתחלה, והוא שיאמר כדעת ישראל הפרשתי, ואם לא אמר טעון גניזה שמא לבו לשמים, ואין מקבלים מהם לחומת ירושלים ולא לאמת המים שבה שנאמר ולכם אין חלק וזכרון בירושלים.

8. If a Gentile donated something to the Temple fund [for the Temple in Jerusalem], they may not accept [it] before the fact, but if they already took it from him, they may not return it to him. If it is something affixed, such as a beam or a stone, they do return it to him so that something permanent will not be in the Holy Temple, as it is said, (Ezra 4:3) *It is not for you and us [to build a House to our God, but we alone will build it].* But in the case of a synagogue, they may accept it right from the start, so long as he says, "I dedicated something with the [same] intention of a Jew," and if he did not say so, it may be preserved in storage in that his intention may be for the sake of heaven. They may not accept anything [from Gentiles] for the walls of Jerusalem or for the water channel there, as it is said, (Nehemiah 2:20) *But you have no share or claim or stake in Jerusalem!*[151]

149. See Babylonian Talmud Arakhin 6b.
150. See Babylonian Talmud Arakhin 6b.
151. See Babylonian Talmud Arakhin 6a.

הלכה ט

אסור לישראל ליטול צדקה מן העכו"ם בפרהסיא, ואם אינו יכול לחיות בצדקה של ישראל ואינו יכול ליטלה מן העכו"ם בצנעה הרי זה מותר, ומלך או שר מן העכו"ם ששלח ממון לישראל לצדקה אין מחזירין אותו לו משום שלום מלכות, אלא נוטלין ממנו וינתן לעניי עכו"ם בסתר כדי שלא ישמע המלך.

9. It is forbidden for a Jew to take *tzedakah* from a Gentile in public, but if he is not able to live on the *tzedakah* of Israel and cannot take *tzedakah* from the Gentiles in private, then he may do so in public. If a king or a noble of the Gentiles sends money to a Jewish community for *tzedakah*, they may not send it back for the sake of the peace of the kingdom, but rather they take it and give it to the poor of the Gentiles in secret so that the king will not hear.[152]

Another situation which would necessitate the public collection of funds was raising money to pay ransom for the redemption of captives. Sometimes rabbis or other figures would be held hostage, and the Jewish community would be asked for ransom money. The community needed to balance the need to save a life with the public welfare. The redemption of captives, because of the obvious threat to life and because of the potential threat to the entire community, took precedence over the regular collection of tzedakah.

הלכה י

פדיון שבויים קודם לפרנסת עניים ולכסותן, ואין לך מצוה גדולה כפדיון שבויים שהשבוי הרי הוא בכלל הרעבים והצמאים והערומים ועומד בסכנת נפשות, והמעלים עיניו מפדיונו הרי זה עובר על לא תאמץ את לבבך ולא תקפוץ את ידך ועל לא תעמוד על דם רעך ועל לא ירדנו בפרך לעיניך, ובטל מצות פתח תפתח את ידך לו, ומצות וחי אחיך עמך, ואהבת לרעך כמוך, והצל לקוחים למות והרבה דברים כאלו, ואין לך מצוה רבה כפדיון שבויים.

10. The redemption of captives held for ransom takes precedence over sustaining the poor and clothing them. You do not find a *mitzvah* greater than the redemption of captives, for captivity is in the same category as famine, drought, or exposure, and one stands in danger to one's life. One who averts his eyes from redeeming [the captive] transgresses [the commandment], (Deut. 15:7) *Do not harden your heart and shut your hand*, and (Lev. 19:16) *Do not stand upon the blood of your neighbor*, and (Lev. 25:53) *He shall not rule ruthlessly over him in your sight*, and nullifies the commandment (Deut. 15:8) *You must open your hand*, and the commandment, (Lev. 25:36) *Let him live by your side as your kinsman*, and (Lev. 19:18) *Love your fellow as yourself*, and (Proverbs 24:11) *If*

152. See Babylonian Talmud Sanhedrin 26b. However, it only states that those who accept charity from Gentiles in public when there is an alternative are ineligible to be witnesses.

you refrained from rescuing those taken off to death, [those condemned to slaughter--if you say, "We knew nothing of it," surely He who fathoms hearts will discern], and many such sayings. You cannot find a greater *mitzvah* than the redemption of captives.[153]

הלכה יא
אנשי העיר שגבו מעות לבנין בית הכנסת ובא להן דבר מצוה מוציאין בו המעות, קנו אבנים וקורות לא ימכרום לדבר מצוה אלא לפדיון שבויים, אע״פ שהביאו את האבנים וגדרום ואת הקורות ופסלום והתקינו הכל לבנין מוכרין הכל לפדיון שבויים בלבד, אבל אם בנו וגמרו לא ימכרו את בית הכנסת אלא יגבו לפדיונן מן הצבור.

11. If people of a city have collected money for the building of a synagogue, and a matter of a *mitzvah* comes before them, they should use the money [for the *mitzvah*]. But if they already purchased stones and beams, they should only sell them in the case of redeeming captives. Even if they have brought the stones and made walls of them, beams and laid them out, they sell it all for the sake of redeeming captives and that alone, but if they have built and completed [the synagogue], they do not sell the synagogue. Rather, they collect for their [the captives'] redemption from the public.[154]

הלכה יב
אין פודין את השבויים ביתר על דמיהן מפני תקון העולם, שלא יהיו האויבים רודפין אחריהם לשבותם, ואין מבריחין את השבויים מפני תקון העולם שלא יהיו האויבים מכבידין עליהן את העול ומרבים בשמירתן.

12. They may not redeem the captives for more than their worth for the sake of civilization, so that the enemies will not pursue after them to enslave them [once they find out they are will to pay anything]. And they do not try to make the captives escape for the sake of civilization, so that the enemies will not increase the weight of their yoke and add more guards.[155]

הלכה יג
מי שמכר עצמו ובניו לעכו״ם או שלוה מהן ושבו אותן או אסרוהו בהלואתן, פעם ראשונה ושנייה מצוה לפדותן, שלישית אין פודין אותן, אבל פודין את הבנים לאחר מיתת אביהן, ואם בקשוהו להורגו פודין אותו מידם אפילו אחר כמה פעמים.

13. He who sells himself and his children to Gentiles or who takes a loan from them and becomes enslaved to them or is imprisoned because of the loan, the first

153. See Babylonian Talmud Bava Batra 8a-b on the importance of redeeming captives and Chullin 7a where Rabbi Phineas ben Yair travels to redeem captives and, on the way, a river parts for him, enabling him to pass through on dry land to fulfill his duty.

154. On the public collection of charity, see Babylonian Talmud Bava Batra 8b.

155. See Mishnah Gittin 4:6. The translation "for the sake of civilization" is used to try to capture the nuance that there is a duty to make the world a less chaotic and dangerous place.

and second time it is a *mitzvah* to redeem them. The third time they do not redeem him, but they redeem the children after the death of their father. But if they want to kill him, then they redeem him from their power, even if this is several times [that this has happened].[156]

הלכה יד
עבד שנשבה הואיל וטבל לשם עבדות וקבל עליו מצות פודין אותו כישראל שנשבה, ושבוי שהמיר לעכו"ם ואפילו למצוה אחת כגון שהיה אוכל נבלה להכעיס וכיוצא בו אסור לפדותו.

14. In the case of a slave who was taken captive, if he immersed himself for the sake of servitude and he accepted upon himself the duty of the *mitzvot*, they redeem him as if he were a Jew who had been taken captive. But if the prisoner rebels and joins the idolators, even if it is by [transgressing] one *mitzvah*, such as the prohibition against eating carrion, in order to infuriate [the Jewish community], etc., it is forbidden to redeem him.[157]

הלכה טו
האשה קודמת לאיש להאכיל ולכסות ולהוציא מבית השבי, מפני שהאיש דרכו לחזר לא האשה ובושתה מרובה, ואם היו שניהם בשביה ונתבעו שניהן לדבר עבירה האיש קודם לפדות לפי שאין דרכו לכך.

15. A woman takes precedence over a man for feeding, clothing, and bringing out of prison, because it is more usual for men to go door to door [to beg] and not for a woman who feels great shame in this. But if both of them [a man and a woman] were in captivity and were in danger of being violated sexually, the man takes precedence for redemption, because this is not the way of things.[158]

הלכה טז
יתום ויתומה שבאו להשיא אותן משיאין האשה קודם לאיש מפני שבושתה של אשה מרובה, ולא יפחתו לה ממשקל ששה דינרים ורביע דינר של כסף טהור, ואם יש בכיס של צדקה נותנין לה לפי כבודה.

16. In the case of a male orphan and a female orphan who come [to the authorities of the community] to get married [but not to each other], the female [orphan] takes precedence over the man, because she feels great shame in this.[159] And they may not give her less than the worth of six and a quarter *dinar* of pure silver, and if they have more in the bank of *tzedakah*, they give to her according to her honor.[160]

---

156. See Babylonian Talmud Gittin 46b-47a.
157. See Babylonian Talmud Gittin 37b and 47a.
158. See Mishnah Horayot 3:7, Babylonian Talmud Ketubot 67a.
159. See Babylonian Talmud Ketubot 67a-b.
160. See Mishnah Ketubot 6:5.

The next two laws take up the theme of trying to create a hierarchy in the value that people have within the community. In law 17, a traditional rabbinic hierarchy is listed, describing people's status according to birth. In the final law, however, this traditional way of thinking is turned on its head, making the value of a person's wisdom or their family closeness the deciding factors. The merit of one's learning and fidelity to family historically took on increasing importance compared to one's lineage.

הלכה יז

היו לפנינו עניים הרבה או שבויים הרבה ואין בכיס כדי לפרנס או כדי לכסות או כדי לפדות את כולן, מקדימין את הכהן ללוי, ולוי לישראל, וישראל לחלל, וחלל לשתוקי, ושתוקי לאסופי, ואסופי לממזר, וממזר לנתין, ונתין לגר, שהנתין גדל עמנו בקדושה, וגר קודם לעבד משוחרר, לפי שהיה בכלל ארור.

17. If we have before us many poor people or many captives, and there is not enough in the fund to sustain them, or to clothe them, or to redeem them all, a priest takes precedence over a Levite, a Levite over a [regular] Jew, a Jew over a *chalel* [an illegitimate child of a priest], a *chalel* over a *shetuki* [an illegitimate child with an unknown father], a *shetuki* over a *asufi* [a foundling], an *asufi* over a *mamzer* [a child who was conceived in a union forbidden by the Torah], a *mamzer* over a *natin* [a descendent of the Gibeonites], and a *natin* over a stranger, so long as the *natin* was praised with us in holiness, and a convert takes precedence over a freed slave, for he [the slave] was once one of the cursed.[161]

הלכה יח

במה דברים אמורים בשהיו שניהן שוין בחכמה, אבל אם היה כהן גדול עם הארץ וממזר תלמיד חכם, תלמיד חכם קודם, וכל הגדול בחכמה קודם את חבירו, ואם היה אחד מהן רבו או אביו אע"פ שיש שם גדול מהן בחכמה, רבו או אביו שהוא תלמיד חכם קודם לזה שהוא גדול מהם בחכמה.

18. To what does this refer? When both who are imprisoned are equal in wisdom. But if there was a High Priest who was an ignoramus and a *mamzer* who was a wise disciple, the wise disciple takes precedence. Anyone who is great in wisdom takes precedence over another. But if one of them [the captives] was one's rabbi or father, even if there is someone who is greater in wisdom, one's rabbi or father [takes precedence]. Even if there is someone there [among the captives] who is greater in wisdom than his rabbi or his father, so long as he [his father or rabbi] is a wise disciple, he [the father or the rabbi] takes precedence over the one who is greater than them in wisdom.[162]

161. See Mishnah Horayot 3:8.

162. See Mishnah Horayot 3:8 and Babylonian Talmud Horayot 13a.

Maimonides now describes the two main institutions for giving tzedakah *in his day, the* kupah *(the "charity coffer") and the* tamchui *(the "charity plate"). Based primarily on the first chapter of the Babylonian Talmud Bava Batra, these practices are both descriptive and prescriptive. Maimonides seems to be describing a standard of support for the poor which the community must uphold.*

הלכה א
כל עיר שיש בה ישראל חייבין להעמיד מהם גבאי צדקה אנשים ידועים ונאמנים שיהיו מחזירין על העם מערב שבת לערב שבת ולוקחין מכל אחד ואחד מה שהוא ראוי ליתן ודבר הקצוב עליו, והן מחלקין המעות מערב שבת לערב שבת ונותנין לכל עני ועני מזונות המספיקין לשבעה ימים, וזו היא הנקרא קופה.

1. Any city in which there is a Jewish community is obligated to raise up collectors of *tzedakah*, people who are well-known and trustworthy, to go door-to-door among the people from Sabbath eve to Sabbath eve and to take from each and every one what is appropriate for them to give. [The amount] should be a set and clear matter for each person. They also distribute the money from Sabbath eve to Sabbath eve and give to each and every poor person enough food to last them for seven days. This method is called the *kupah* [the "coffer" for the charity fund].[163]

הלכה ב
וכן מעמידין גבאין שלוקחין בכל יום ויום מכל חצר וחצר פת ומיני מאכל או פירות או מעות ממי שמתנדב לפי שעה, ומחלקין את הגבוי לערב בין העניים ונותנין לכל עני ממנו פרנסת יומו, וזהו הנקרא תמחוי.

2. So also [the community] must enlist collectors to take [donations] on a day-to-day basis, from each and every yard, a main dish, other types of food, fruit, or money for anyone who would donate something at that time, and they distribute this collection in the evening among the poor and give to each poor person from it a day's sustenance. This method is called the *tamchui* [the "charity plate"].

הלכה ג
מעולם לא ראינו ולא שמענו בקהל מישראל שאין להן קופה של צדקה, אבל תמחוי יש מקומות שנהגו בו ויש מקומות שלא נהגו בו, והמנהג הפשוט היום שיהיו גבאי הקופה מחזירין בכל יום ומחלקין מערב שבת לערב שבת.

3. Never have we seen or heard of a Jewish community that does not have a *kupah*, but as for a *tamchui*, there are places whose custom it is to have it and places that do not. The widespread custom today is that the collectors of the

163. For laws 1-12, see Babylonian Talmud Bava Batra 8a-11b in addition to the citations listed below.

kupah make their rounds each day [to collect the *tzedakah*], and they distribute it on each Sabbath eve.[164]

הלכה ד
בתעניות מחלקים מזונות לעניים, וכל תענית שאכלו העם ולנו ולא חלקו צדקה לעניים הרי אלו כשופכי דמים ועליהם נאמר בקבלה צדק ילין בה ועתה מרצחים, במה דברים אמורים בשלא נתנו להן הפת והפירות שאוכלים בהם הפת כגון תמרים וענבים, אבל אם אחרו המעות או החטים אינן כשופכי דמים.

4. On fast days, they must still distribute food for the poor. Any fast where the community eats [at the end after sundown], goes to sleep, and did not distribute *tzedakah* to the poor is like [a community] that sheds blood. About them it is written in the prophetic books, (Isaiah 1:21) *Where righteousness [tzedek] dwelt, but now murderers.* To what does this refer? When they have not given them a main dish and fruit with which to eat it, such as dates or grapes. But if the money or the wheat was delayed [and they did not give them food because of a mitigating circumstance], then they are not like murderers.[165]

הלכה ה
הקופה אינה נגבית אלא בשנים שאין עושים שררה על הצבור בממון פחות משנים, ומותר להאמין לאחד המעות של קופה, ואינה נחלקת אלא בשלשה מפני שהיא כדיני ממונות, שנותנים לכל אחד די מחסורו לשבת, והתמחוי נגבה בשלשה שאינו דבר קצוב, ומתחלק בשלשה.

5. The *kupah* may only be collected by two individuals, for there is no authority to an institution in the community in financial matters except if there are at least two people [to run it], but it is permissible to entrust one person with the money from the *kupah*. It may only be distributed by three individuals, because it is as if they are making judicial decisions about money [and a Jewish court is comprised of three individuals], for they give to each one enough to fill this lack for the Sabbath [and this is a matter of judgment]. And the *tamchui* is collected by three, for this is not a clearly defined matter [and also requires judicial decisions], and it is distributed by three.[166]

הלכה ו
התמחוי נגבה בכל יום, והקופה מערב שבת לערב שבת, והתמחוי לעניי עולם, והקופה לעניי אותה העיר בלבד.

6. The *tamchui* is collected each day, and the *kupah* [is collected] each Sabbath eve. The *tamchui* is given to the poor everywhere, and the *kupah* is given to [the poor of] that city alone.

---

164. See also Babylonian Talmud Sanhedrin 17b on the basic requirements for a community.
165. See Babylonian Talmud Sanhedrin 35a.
166. See Mishnah Péah 8:7.

הלכה ז
רשאין בני העיר לעשות קופה תמחוי, ותמחוי קופה, ולשנותן לכל מה שירצו מצרכי צבור, ואע״פ שלא התנו כן בשעה שגבו, ואם היה במדינה חכם גדול שהכל גובין על דעתו והוא יחלק לעניים כפי מה שיראה, הרי זה רשאי לשנותן לכל מה שיראה לו מצרכי צבור.

7. The citizens of the city are permitted to interchange the *kupah* and the *tamchui* one with the other, and they may exchange them according to the desire fitting the needs of the community, even though they did not stipulate such at the time it was collected. If there is someone in the province who is especially wise, everything should be collected according to his understanding, and he should distribute it as he sees best. This person is permitted to exchange them [the *kupah* and the *tamchui*] as he sees fit according to the needs of the community.

Maimonides now changes the focus half-way through this chapter and explains the rules for the collectors of tzedakah. *The task of collecting* tzedakah *was extremely praiseworthy but also required effort to avoid even the appearance of wrong-doing. In addition, Maimonides explicates factors that might affect one's need for community support, including traveling between communities or pressure to sell one's property during a difficult market.*

הלכה ח
גבאי צדקה אין רשאין לפרוש זה מזה בשוק, אלא כדי שיהיה זה פורש לשער וזה פורש לחנות וגובין.

8. Collectors of *tzedakah* are not permitted to spread out far from each other [while collecting] in the market [so as to avoid suspicion], except when one goes through a gate while the other goes into a store so they may make a collection.

הלכה ט
מצא הגבאי מעות בשוק לא יתנם לתוך כיסו אלא לתוך ארנקי של צדקה וכשיגיע לביתו יטלם.

9. If a *tzedakah* collector finds money in the market, he may not put it in his pocket [so it looks like he is stealing], but rather he puts it in the money bag of the *tzedakah*, and when he gets home he may take it out.

הלכה י
היה הגבאי נושה בחבירו מנה ופרעו בשוק לא יתנם לתוך כיסו, אלא לתוך ארנקי של צדקה, וכשיגיע לביתו יטלם, ולא ימנה מעות הקופה שנים שנים אלא אחד אחד מפני החשד שנאמר והייתם נקיים מה׳ ומישראל.

10. If a *tzedakah* collector engages in business with another in the market [while he is collecting *tzedakah*] and he [the other person] pays him [the collector in front of others], he may not place [the money] in his pocket, but rather he puts it in the money bag of *tzedakah*, and when he gets home he may take it out. He may also not count the money from the *kupah* two by two but rather one coin at a time so that there is no suspicion, as it is said, (Num. 32:22) *You shall be clear before the Eternal and before Israel.*

הלכה יא

גבאי צדקה שאין להם עניים לחלק מצרפין המעות דינרין לאחרים אבל לא לעצמן, גבאי תמחוי שאין להם עניים לחלק מוכרים לאחרים ואין מוכרים לעצמם, ואין מחשבים בצדקה עם גבאי צדקה, ולא בהקדש עם הגזברין, שנאמר אך לא יחשב אתם הכסף הנתן על ידם כי באמונה הם עושים.

11. If the collectors of *tzedakah* do not have poor people [at that moment] to whom to distribute, they may combine the money into *dinarim*, for the sake of others but not for themselves. The collectors of the *tamchui* who do not have poor people to whom to distribute may sell [donated gifts] for the sake of others but not for their own sake. People should not investigate the collectors of *tzedakah*, the treasurer of the Temple, [that is, demand a list of who gave what,] as it is said, (II Kings 22:7) *However, no check is to be kept on them for the silver that is delivered to them, for they deal honestly.*

הלכה יב

מי שישב במדינה שלשים יום כופין אותו ליתן צדקה לקופה עם בני המדינה, ישב שם שלשה חדשים כופין אותו ליתן התמחוי, ישב שם ששה חדשים כופין אותו ליתן צדקה בכסות שמכסים בה עניי העיר, ישב שם תשעה חדשים כופין אותו ליתן צדקה לקבורה שקוברין בה את העניים ועושין להם כל צרכי קבורה.

12. If someone stays in a province for thirty days, they may coerce him to give *tzedakah* for the *kupah* for the citizens of that province. If he stays for three months, they may coerce him to give to the *tamchui*. If he stays for six months, they may coerce him to give *tzedakah* for clothing, so they may clothe the poor of that city. If he stays for nine months, they may coerce him to give *tzedakah* for burial, so they may bury the poor and take care of all of the needs for burial.

הלכה יג

מי שיש לו מזון שתי סעודות אסור לו ליטול מן התמחוי, היו לו מזון ארבע עשרה סעודות לא יטול מן הקופה, היו לו מאתים זוז אע"פ שאינו נושא ונותן בהם]או שיש לו חמשים זוז ונושא ונותן בהם[הרי זה לא יטול לקט שכחה ופאה ומעשר עני, היו לו מאתים חסר דינר אפילו אלף נותנין לו כאחד הרי זה מותר ליקח, היו בידו מעות והרי הן עליו חוב או שהיו ממושכנים לכתובת אשתו הרי זה מותר ליקח.

13. One who has enough food for two meals is forbidden to take from the *tamchui*. If one has food for fourteen meals, he may not take from the *kupah*.[167] If he had 200 *zuz* and does not engage in business with them, or if he had fifty *zuz* and does engage in business with them, then he may not take *leket*, *shikhecha*, *péah*, and *ma'esar ani*. If he had 199 *dinar*, even if a thousand people gave him at once, he is permitted to take [everything]. If he had money in his possession but he has a debt or this is collateral for the prenuptial agreement [*ketubah*] for his wife, then he is permitted to take [*tzedakah*].[168]

---

167. See Babylonian Talmud Shabbat 118a.
168. See Mishnah Péah 8:7.

הלכה יד

עני שצריך ויש לו חצר וכלי בית אפילו היו לו כלי כסף וכלי זהב אין מחייבין אותו למכור את ביתו ואת כלי תשמישו אלא מותר ליקח, ומצוה ליתן לו, במה דברים אמורים בכלי אכילה ושתיה ומלבוש ומצעות וכיוצא בהן, אבל אם היו כלי כסף וכלי זהב כגון מגרדת או עלי וכיוצא בהן מוכרן ולוקח פחות מהן, במה דברים אמורים קודם שיגיע לגבות מן העם, אבל אחר שגבה הצדקה מחייבים אותו למכור כליו וליקח אחרים פחותין מהם ואחר כך יטול.

14. If a poor person is in need who owns a yard and household utensils, even if they are made of silver or gold, they may not require him to sell his home or his utensils, but rather he is permitted to take [*tzedakah*], and it is a *mitzvah* to give to him. In what situation does this apply? To utensils for eating, drinking, doing laundry, for bedding, and similar such things. But if the utensils of silver and gold are things such as a trowel or a pestle or something similar, he must sell them and he gets [utensils] of lesser value. When does this apply [that they force him to sell extraneous tools]? Before he has collected [*tzedakah*] from the people. But even after he has collected *tzedakah*, they still make him sell his utensils and take others of lesser value, and then afterwards he may take [*tzedakah* again].[169]

הלכה טו

בעל הבית שהיה מהלך לעיר ותמו לו המעות בדרך ואין לו עתה מה יאכל הרי זה מותר ליקח לקט שכחה ופאה ומעשר עני וליהנות מן הצדקה, ולכשיגיע לביתו אינו חייב לשלם שהרי עני היה באותה שעה, הא למה זה דומה לעני שהעשיר שאינו חייב לשלם.

15. If a owner of a home was traveling to a city and lost his money while on the way and now has nothing to eat, then he is permitted to take *leket*, *shikhecha*, *péah*, *ma'esar ani*, and to benefit from *tzedakah*. And when he arrives at his home, he does not need to pay [the money back], for he was a poor person at that time. To what is this similar? To a poor person who becomes rich and does not need to pay [back all the money that sustained him while he was poor].[170]

הלכה טז

מי שהיו לו בתים שדות וכרמים ואם מוכרן בימי הגשמים מוכרן בזול ואם הניחן עד ימות החמה מוכרן בשויהן, אין מחייבין אותו למכור אלא מאכילין אותו מעשר עני עד חצי דמיהן ולא ידחוק עצמו וימכור שלא בזמן מכירה.

16. If one owns houses, fields, or vineyards, and if he sold them during the rainy season, it would be at a loss, whereas if he waited until the dry season, he could sell them for their worth, in such a case, they may not require him to sell [when he would lose money], but rather they feed him from *ma'esar ani* up until half their

169. See Babylonian Talmud Ketubot 68a.

170. See Mishnah Péah 5:4.

[his property's] worth,[171] and they do not pressure him to sell at a time when it would be disadvantageous to sell.

הלכה יז

היו שאר האדם לוקחין ביוקר והוא אינו מוצא שיקח ממנו אלא בזול מפני שהוא דחוק וטרוד אין מחייבין אותו למכור, אלא אוכל מעשר עני והולך עד שימכור בשוה וידעו הכל שאינו דחוק למכור.

17. If the rest of the people are buying at high prices, and he finds that no one will buy from him except at a cheap price because he is under pressure and in dire straits, they may not require him to sell [at that time]. Rather, he eats from *ma'esar ani* and continues until he can sell for their value, as everyone knows so he is not under pressure to sell [at a loss].[172]

הלכה יח

עני שגבו לו כדי להשלים מחסורו והותירו על מה שהוא צריך הרי המותר שלו, ומותר עניים לעניים, ומותר שבויים לשבויים, מותר שבוי לאותו שבוי, מותר מתים למתים, מותר המת ליורשיו.

18. If they collected money for a certain poor person in order to fill his lack, and they accumulated a surplus [by collecting more than what he was lacking], the surplus belongs to him. And so if they collected a surplus for poor people in general, [the surplus is set aside] for the poor [in the future]. And so a surplus for captives [is set aside for future] captives, and so for a specific captive, [the surplus goes to] that specific captive. And so a surplus for taking care of the dead in general [is set aside for the future needs of] taking care of the dead, and so if there is a surplus [that they collected] for a specific dead person, it goes to his heirs.[173]

הלכה יט

עני שנתן פרוטה לתמחוי או פרוטה לקופה מקבלים ממנו, ואם לא נתן אין מחייבין אותו ליתן, נתנו לו בגדים חדשים והחזיר להן את השחקין מקבלין ממנו, ואם לא נתן אין מחייבין אותו ליתן.

19. A poor person who has given a *perutah* to the *tamchui* or to the *kupah*, they accept it from him. If he did not give [anything], they do not require him to give. If they gave him new clothes, and he returned the worn garments, they accept them from him. And if he did not donate [to the *kupah*], they do not require him to give.[174]

---

171. See Babylonian Talmud Bava Kama 7a.

172. See Babylonian Talmud Bava Kamma 7a-b. It is remarkable, however, that the Talmud teaches the opposite of Maimonides' ruling. However, later legal decisions are in accordance with Maimonides, perhaps suggesting a problem with the transmission of texts.

173. See Mishnah Shekalim 2:5.

174. See Tosefta Péah 4:10.

Maimonides begins this final chapter with motivational reasons to give tzedakah, *both of a theological and practical nature. He continually invokes the values of integrity, kinship, virtue, and dignity. For an in-depth analysis of this chapter, see the Introduction.*

הלכה א
חייבין אנו להזהר במצות צדקה יותר מכל מצות עשה, שהצדקה סימן לצדיק זרע אברהם אבינו שנאמר כי ידעתיו למען אשר יצוה את בניו לעשות צדקה, ואין כסא ישראל מתכונן ודת האמת עומדת אלא בצדקה שנאמר בצדקה תכונני, ואין ישראל נגאלין אלא בצדקה שנאמר ציון במשפט תפדה ושביה בצדקה.

1. We must be especially careful to observe the *mitzvah* of *tzedakah*, more so than any other positive *mitzvah*, for *tzedakah* is a sign of the righteous [*tzadik*] lineage of Abraham, our father, as it is said, (Genesis 18:19) *For I have singled him out, that he may instruct his children and his posterity [to keep the way of the Eternal] by doing what is just [tzedakah].*[175] The throne of Israel is established and the religion of truth stands only on tzedakah, as it is said, (Isaiah 54:14) *You shall be established through righteousness [tzedek].* And Israel will only be redeemed through *tzedakah*, as it is said, (Isaiah 1:27) *Zion shall be saved in the judgment; her repentant ones, in the retribution [tzedakah].*[176]

הלכה ב
לעולם אין אדם מעני מן הצדקה ואין דבר רע ולא היזק נגלל בשביל הצדקה שנאמר והיה מעשה הצדקה שלום, כל המרחם מרחמין עליו שנאמר ונתן לך רחמים ורחמך והרבך, וכל מי שהוא אכזרי ואינו מרחם יש לחוש ליחסו, שאין האכזריות מצויה אלא בעכו"ם שנאמר אכזרי המה ולא ירחמו, וכל ישראל והנלוה עליהם כאחים הם שנאמר בנים אתם לה' אלהיכם ואם לא ירחם האח על האח מי ירחם עליו, ולמי עניי ישראל נושאין עיניהן, הלעכו"ם ששונאין אותו ורודפים אחריהן הא אין עיניהן תלויות אלא לאחיהן.

2. Never has anyone become poor by giving to *tzedakah*, nor has anything bad ever come of it, nor has any harm occurred because of *tzedakah*, as it is said, (Isaiah 32:17) *The work of righteousness [tzedakah] is peace.* Anyone who shows compassion, others will show compassion to him, as it is said, (Deut. 13:18) *[May God] show you compassion, and let your compassion increase.*[177] And if someone is cruel and without compassion, then his lineage is suspect, for cruelty is only found among the idolatrous nations, as it is said, (Jer. 50:42) *They*

175. See Babylonian Talmud Yevamot 79a.
176. See Babylonian Talmud Shabbat 139a.
177. This is a play on the text. The original reads, "and in His compassion increase you," that is, God will multiply your descendants. Here, the compassion itself increases.

are cruel, they show no mercy.[178] All Israel and all who are associated with them are like brothers, as it is said, (Deut. 14:1) *You are children of the Eternal your God.*[179] And if a brother does not show compassion for another brother, then who will have compassion for him? And to whom can the poor of Israel look? To the idolatrous nations that hate them and pursue them? They can only look to rely upon their brothers.

הלכה ג

כל המעלים עיניו מן הצדקה הרי זה נקרא בליעל כמו שנקרא עובד עכו"ם בליעל, ובעכו"ם הוא אומר יצאו אנשים בני בליעל ובמעלים עיניו מן הצדקה הוא אומר השמר לך פן יהיה דבר עם לבבך בליעל, ונקרא רשע שנאמר ורחמי רשעים אכזרי, ונקרא חוטא שנאמר וקרא עליך אל ה' והיה בך חטא, והקב"ה קרוב לשועת עניים שנאמר שועת עניים אתה תשמע, לפיכך צריך להזהר בצעקתם שהרי ברית כרותה להם שנאמר והיה כי יצעק אלי ושמעתי כי חנון אני.

3. Anyone who averts his eyes from [the need of] *tzedakah* is called *Belial* ["Wickedness"], just as the idolators worship *Belial*, and of the idolators Scripture says, (Deut. 13:14) *That some scoundrels [children of Belial] from among you have gone [and subverted the inhabitants of their town]* by averting their eyes from [the need of] *tzedakah*. It says, (Deut. 15:9) *Beware lest you harbor a base [belial] thought.*[180] And such a person is called, "wicked," as it is said, (Prov. 12:10) *The compassion of the wicked is cruelty.* Such a person is called, "a sinner," as it is said, (Deut. 15:9) *He will cry out to the Eternal against you, and you will incur a sin.*[181] The Holy One, Blessed Be He, is close to the cries of the poor, as it is said, (Job 34:28) *He listens to the cry of the needy.*[182] Therefore, one needs to be especially sensitive to their cries, for they [the poor] have a covenant established [between them and God], as it is said, (Exodus 22:26) *Therefore, if he cries out to Me, I will pay heed, for I am compassionate.*

הלכה ד

כל הנותן צדקה לעני בסבר פנים רעות ופניו כבושות בקרקע אפילו נתן לו אלף זהובים אבד זכותו והפסידה, אלא נותן לו בסבר פנים יפות ובשמחה ומתאונן עמו על צרתו שנאמר אם לא בכיתי לקשה יום עגמה נפשי לאביון, ומדבר לו דברי תחנונים ונחומים שנאמר ולב אלמנה ארנין.

4. Anyone who gives *tzedakah* to a poor person with a scowl and causes him to be embarrassed,[183] even if he gave him a thousand *zuz*, has destroyed and lost any merit thereby. Rather, one should give cheerfully, with happiness [to do so] and empathy for his plight, as it is said, (Job 30:25) *Did I not weep for the unfortunate? Did I not grieve for the needy?* And one should speak to him words

---

178. See Babylonian Talmud Shabbat 151b.
179. See Babylonian Talmud Bava Batra 10a and the Introduction.
180. See Babylonian Talmud Ketubot 68a.
181. See Babylonian Talmud Bava Batra 10a. The translation reads, "guilt," but the connection here is through "sin."
182. Maimonides does not quote this exactly.
183. Literally: causes his face to fall in shame.

of comfort and consolation, as it is said, (Job 29:13) *[I received the blessing of the lost,] I gladdened the heart of the widow.*

הלכה ה

שאל העני ממך ואין בידך כלום ליתן לו פייסהו בדברים, ואסור לגעור בעני או להגביה קולו עליו בצעקה, מפני שלבו נשבר ונדכא והרי הוא אומר לב נשבר ונדכה אלהים לא תבזה, ואומר להחיות רוח שפלים ולהחיות לב נדכאים, ואוי למי שהכלים את העני אוי לו, אלא יהיה לו כאב בין ברחמים בין בדברים שנאמר אב אנכי לאביונים.

5. If a poor person asks of you [to give him something], and you do not have anything in your possession to give to him, comfort him with words.[184] It is forbidden to speak harshly to a poor person or to raise your voice in a shout, for his heart is broken and crushed. Thus it says in Scripture, (Psalms 51:19) *God, You will not despise a contrite and crushed heart.* And it says, (Isaiah 57:15) *Reviving the spirits of the lowly, reviving the hearts of the contrite.* And woe to anyone who shames a poor person! Woe to him! Rather, let him be like a father to him, in compassion and in words, as it is said, (Job 29:15) *I was a father to the needy.*

הלכה ו

הכופה אחרים ליתן צדקה ומעשה אותן שכרו גדול משכר הנותן שנאמר והיה מעשה הצדקה שלום, ועל גבאי צדקה וכיוצא בהם אומר ומצדיקי הרבים ככוכבים.

6. One who coerces others to give *tzedakah* is considered to have performed even a greater deed then the person who actually gives, as it is said, (Isaiah 32:17) *For the work of the righteousness [tzedakah] shall be peace, [and the effect of righteousness [tzedakah], calm and confidence forever.]*[185] Of collectors of *tzedakah* and similar people it is written, (Daniel 12:3) *Those who lead the many to righteousness [matzdiké harabim] will be like the stars [forever and ever].*

The next eight passages are often presented as a text all to themselves, the "Eight Levels of Tzedakah.*" They are presented in descending order from the best way to give to the needy to the worst.*

הלכה ז

שמנה מעלות יש בצדקה זו למעלה מזו, מעלה גדולה שאין למעלה ממנה זה המחזיק ביד ישראל שמך ונותן לו מתנה או הלואה או עושה עמו שותפות או ממציא לו מלאכה כדי לחזק את ידו עד שלא יצטרך לבריות לשאול, ועל זה נאמר והחזקת בו גר ותושב וחי עמך כלומר החזק בו עד שלא יפול ויצטרך.

7. There are eight levels of *tzedakah*, each one greater than the other. The greatest level, higher than all the rest, is to fortify a fellow Jew and give him a

184. See Leviticus Rabbah 34:15 as well as Babylonian Talmud Bava Batra 9b.

185. See Babylonian Talmud Bava Batra 9a. The first half of the verse refers to the one who gives. The second part of the verse refers to one who coerces others and whose reward is more lasting.

gift, a loan, form with him a partnership, or find work for him, until he is strong enough so that he does not need to ask others [for sustenance]. Of this it is said, (Lev. 25:35) *[If your kinsman, being in straits, comes under your authority,] and you hold him as though a resident alien, let him live by your side.* That is as if to say, "*Hold* him up," so that he will not fall and be in need.[186]

הלכה ח

פחות מזה הנותן צדקה לעניים ולא ידע למי נתן ולא ידע העני ממי לקח, שהרי זו מצוה לשמה, כגון לשכת חשאים שהיתה במקדש, שהיו הצדיקים נותנין בה בחשאי והעניים בני טובים מתפרנסין ממנה בחשאי, וקרוב לזה הנותן לתוך קופה של צדקה, ולא יתן אדם לתוך קופה של צדקה אלא אם כן יודע שהממונה נאמן וחכם ויודע להנהיג כשורה כר׳ חנניה בן תרדיון.

8. One level lower than this is one who gives *tzedakah* to the poor and does not know to whom he gives, and the poor person does not know from whom he receives.[187] This is purely a *mitzvah* for its own sake, such as the Chamber of Secrets in the Holy Temple, for there the righteous would give in secret [and leave], and the poor, of good background, would sustain themselves from it in secret. Very close to this is one who gives to the *kupah* of *tzedakah*, but one should not contribute to the *kupah* of *tzedakah* unless one is certain that the one who counts it is trustworthy and wise and behaves competently, as was Rabbi Chanania ben Teradion.[188]

הלכה ט

פחות מזה שידע הנותן למי יתן ולא ידע העני ממי לקח, כגון גדולי החכמים שהיו הולכין בסתר ומשליכין המעות בפתחי העניים, וכזה ראוי לע׳שות ומעלה טובה היא אם אין הממונין בצדקה נוהגין כשורה.

9. One level lower is one who gives *tzedakah* and the giver knows to whom he gives but the poor person does not know from whom he takes. Such did the great sages who would go in secret and throw money onto the doorways of the poor.[189] A method such as this one is a good way when the keepers of *tzedakah* do not behave competently.

186. See Babylonian Talmud Shabbat 63a.

187. Maimonides holds the anonymity of both giver and receiver of great importance, but he does not require anonymity at the highest level of giving. This is perhaps because the highest level of giving addresses the source of poverty whereas giving something to a beggar only alleviates a person's temporary need. Preventing poverty is therefore of such importance that anonymity becomes secondary in that instance.

188. See Babylonian Talmud Bava Batra 10b and Avodah Zarah 17b. Rabbi Chanania ben Teradion had a reputation for competence and honesty, so he dealt with the collection and distribution of charity funds. He was later tortured and executed by the Romans.

189. See Babylonian Talmud Ketubot 67b.

הלכה י

פחות מזה שידע העני ממי נטל ולא ידע הנותן, כגון גדולי החכמים שהיו צוררים המעות בסדיניהן ומפשילין לאחוריהן ובאין העניים ונוטלין כדי שלא יהיה להן בושה.

10. One level lower is when the poor person knows from whom he takes but the giver does not know to whom he gives. Such was the way of the sages who would tie coins to their garments and would throw the bundle over their shoulder so the poor could come up [behind them] and take [them] without being embarrassed.[190]

הלכה יא

פחות מזה שיתן לו בידו קודם שישאל.

11. One level lower is to give to him with one's own hand before he can ask.[191]

הלכה יב

פחות מזה שיתן לו אחר שישאל.

12. One level lower is to give to him after he has asked.

הלכה יג

פחות מזה שיתן לו פחות מן הראוי בסבר פנים יפות.

13. One level lower is to give him less than one should but with kindness.

הלכה יד

פחות מזה שיתן לו בעצב.

14. One level lower is to give to him begrudgingly.

Maimonides concludes this treatise by giving examples of the ideal ways of giving tzedakah. *Giving to the poor is understood to be a holy act, and God's presence is manifest in the face of the poor person who receives* tzedakah. *Maimonides also implies a tension in the act of receiving* tzedakah, *namely, that one should do everything in one's power not to become dependent upon the community, but at the same time one should not endanger oneself and refuse the community's help when necessary.*

הלכה טו

גדולי החכמים היו נותנין פרוטה לעני קודם כל תפלה ואחר כך מתפללין שנאמר אני בצדק אחזה פניך.

15. The greatest among the sages used to give a *perutah* to the poor before every prayer service and only afterwards would they pray, as it is said, (Psalms 17:15) *Then I, justified [betzedek], will behold Your face.*[192]

---

190. See Babylonian Talmud Ketubot 67b.

191. It can be assumed that from this point on the situation is one of face to face encounter, handing something to another.

192. See Babylonian Talmud Bava Batra 10a.

הלכה טז
הנותן מזונות לבניו ולבנותיו הגדולים שאינו חייב במזונותיהן כדי ללמד הזכרים תורה ולהנהיג הבנות בדרך ישרה ולא יהיו מבוזות, וכן הנותן מזונות לאביו ולאמו הרי זה בכלל הצדקה, וצדקה גדולה היא שהקרוב קודם, וכל המאכיל ומשקה עניים ויתומים על שלחנו הרי זה קורא אל ה׳ ויענהו ומתענג שנאמר אז תקרא וה׳ יענה.

16. One should give sustenance to one's sons and daughters who have come of age and to whom one is no longer required to give such support so that they may study the testimonies of Torah and to guide one's daughters on an upright path and not become shameful.[193] So also one should give sustenance to one's father and mother, for this is essential *tzedakah*. It is an important principle of *tzedakah* that a relative takes precedence [over another].[194] All who give food and drink to the poor and the orphans from his own table can call to God and he will be answered with joy, as it is said, (Isaiah 58:9) *Then, when you call, the Eternal will answer.*

הלכה יז
צוו חכמים שיהיו בני ביתו של אדם עניים ויתומים במקום העבדים, מוטב לו להשתמש באלו ויהנו בני אברהם יצחק ויעקב מנכסיו ולא יהנו בהם זרע חם, שכל המרבה עבדים בכל יום ויום מוסיף חטא ועון בעולם, ואם יהיו עניים בני ביתו בכל שעה ושעה מוסיף זכיות ומצות.

17. The sages commanded that the poor and orphans should be members of one's household instead of servants. It is better to use their services [by employing them] and that the children of Abraham, Isaac, and Jacob benefit from one's property and not the descendants of Ham, for one who increases the number of servants each and every day adds to the sin and iniquity of the world. But if the poor are made members of one's household, each and every hour one adds merit and *mitzvot*.[195]

הלכה יח
לעולם ידחוק אדם עצמו ויתגלגל בצער ואל יצטרך לבריות ואל ישליך עצמו על הצבור, וכן צוו חכמים ואמרו עשה שבתך חול ואל תצטרך לבריות, ואפילו היה חכם ומכובד והעני יעסוק באומנות ואפילו באומנות מנוולת ולא יצטרך לבריות, מוטב לפשוט עור בהמות נבלות ולא יאמר לעם חכם גדול אני כהן אני פרנסוני, ובכך צוו חכמים, גדולי החכמים היו מהם חוטבי עצים ונושאי הקורות ושואבי מים לגנות ועושי הברזל והפחמים ולא שאלו מן הצבור ולא קיבלו מהם כשנתנו להם.

18. One should always strain oneself and endure hardship and not come to depend on others rather than cast oneself onto the community. Thus the sages

193. See Babylonian Talmud Ketubot 50a.
194. See Babylonian Talmud Bava Metzia 71a.
195. See Pirké Avot 1:5, 2:7.

commanded, "Make your Sabbaths into weekdays rather than come to depend on others."[196]

Even if one is wise and revered and becomes poor, he should engage in some kind of craft, even a menial one, rather than come to depend on others. Better to stretch leather from carrion than to say, "I am a great sage," [or] "I am a priest: Feed me." Thus have the sages commanded. Great sages were splitters of wood, raisers of beams, drawers of water for gardens, iron workers, and blacksmiths rather than ask [for their living] from the community or accept anything when they gave to them.

הלכה יט

כל מי שאינו צריך ליטול ומרמה את העם ונוטל אינו מת מן הזקנה עד שיצטרך לבריות, והרי הוא בכלל ארור הגבר אשר יבטח באדם, וכל מי שצריך ליטול ואינו יכול לחיות אלא אם כן נוטל כגון זקן או חולה או בעל יסורין ומגיס דעתו ואינו נוטל הרי זה שופך דמים ומתחייב בנפשו ואין לו בצערו אלא חטאות ואשמות, וכל מי שצריך ליטול וציער ודחק את השעה וחיה חיי צער כדי שלא יטריח על הצבור אינו מת מן הזקנה עד שיפרנס אחרים משלו, ועליו ועל כל כיוצא בזה נאמר ברוך הגבר אשר יבטח בה׳. סליקו להו הלכות מתנות עניים בס״ד.

19. Anyone who does not need [*tzedakah*] but deceives people and takes will not reach death in old age without having come to depend upon others [in reality].[197] For such a one fits the type: (Jer. 17:5) *Cursed is he who trusts in man* [and does not heed divine providence]. And anyone who needs to take [*tzedakah*] and cannot live without it unless he takes, such as an elderly person, a sick person, or one who has many afflictions, but whose mind is full of pride and will not take is like one who sheds blood, is guilty of his own death, and gets nothing for his hardship except sins and guilt. But anyone who needs to take and endures hardship, presses himself, and lives a life of hardship so as not to burden the community will not reach death in old age without being able to sustain others from his wealth. Of him and those like him it is written, (Jer. 17:7) *Blessed is he who trusts in the Eternal.*

Thus ends, with the help of God, the laws on gifts for the poor.

196. See Babylonian Talmud Pesachim 112a.

197. See Mishnah Péah 8:9 and Babylonian Talmud Ketubot 68a.

Appendix I: Sources from the Torah on *Tzedakah*

Leviticus 19:9-10

וּבְקֻצְרְכֶם אֶת־קְצִיר אַרְצְכֶם לֹא תְכַלֶּה פְּאַת שָׂדְךָ לִקְצֹר וְלֶקֶט קְצִירְךָ לֹא תְלַקֵּט׃ וְכַרְמְךָ לֹא תְעוֹלֵל
וּפֶרֶט כַּרְמְךָ לֹא תְלַקֵּט לֶעָנִי וְלַגֵּר תַּעֲזֹב אֹתָם אֲנִי יְהוָה אֱלֹהֵיכֶם׃

When you reap the harvest of your land, you shall not reap all the way to the edges of your field, or gather the gleanings of your harvest. You shall not pick your vineyard bare, or gather the separated fruit of your vineyard; you shall leave them for the poor and the stranger: I the Eternal am your God.

Leviticus 23:22

וּבְקֻצְרְכֶם אֶת־קְצִיר אַרְצְכֶם לֹא־תְכַלֶּה פְּאַת שָׂדְךָ בְּקֻצְרֶךָ וְלֶקֶט קְצִירְךָ לֹא תְלַקֵּט לֶעָנִי וְלַגֵּר תַּעֲזֹב
אֹתָם אֲנִי יְהוָה אֱלֹהֵיכֶם׃

And when you reap the harvest of your land, you shall not reap all the way to the edges of the field, or gather the gleanings of your harvest; you shall leave them for the poor and the stranger: I the Eternal am your God.

Leviticus 25:35-38

וְכִי־יָמוּךְ אָחִיךָ וּמָטָה יָדוֹ עִמָּךְ וְהֶחֱזַקְתָּ בּוֹ גֵּר וְתוֹשָׁב וָחַי עִמָּךְ׃ אַל־תִּקַּח מֵאִתּוֹ נֶשֶׁךְ וְתַרְבִּית וְיָרֵאתָ
מֵאֱלֹהֶיךָ וְחֵי אָחִיךָ עִמָּךְ׃ אֶת־כַּסְפְּךָ לֹא־תִתֵּן לוֹ בְּנֶשֶׁךְ וּבְמַרְבִּית לֹא־תִתֵּן אָכְלֶךָ׃ אֲנִי יְהוָה אֱלֹהֵיכֶם
אֲשֶׁר־הוֹצֵאתִי אֶתְכֶם מֵאֶרֶץ מִצְרָיִם לָתֵת לָכֶם אֶת־אֶרֶץ כְּנַעַן לִהְיוֹת לָכֶם לֵאלֹהִים׃

If your kinsman, being in straits, comes under your authority, and you hold him as though a resident alien, let him live by your side: do not exact from him advance or accrued interest, but fear your God. Let him live by your side as your kinsman. Do not lend him money at advance interest, or give him your food at accrued interest. I the Eternal am your God, who led you out of the land of Egypt, to give you the land of Canaan, to be your God.

Deuteronomy 14:28-29

מִקְצֵה שָׁלֹשׁ שָׁנִים תּוֹצִיא אֶת־כָּל־מַעְשַׂר תְּבוּאָתְךָ בַּשָּׁנָה הַהִוא וְהִנַּחְתָּ בִּשְׁעָרֶיךָ׃ וּבָא הַלֵּוִי כִּי אֵין־לוֹ
חֵלֶק וְנַחֲלָה עִמָּךְ וְהַגֵּר וְהַיָּתוֹם וְהָאַלְמָנָה אֲשֶׁר בִּשְׁעָרֶיךָ וְאָכְלוּ וְשָׂבֵעוּ לְמַעַן יְבָרֶכְךָ יְהוָה אֱלֹהֶיךָ
בְּכָל־מַעֲשֵׂה יָדְךָ אֲשֶׁר תַּעֲשֶׂה׃

Every third year you shall bring out the full tithe of your yield of that year, but leave it within your settlements. Then the Levite, who has no hereditary portion as you have, and the stranger, the fatherless, and the widow in your settlements shall come and eat their fill, so that the Eternal your God may bless you in all the enterprises you undertake.

Deuteronomy 15:1-11

מִקֵּץ שֶׁבַע־שָׁנִים תַּעֲשֶׂה שְׁמִטָּה׃ וְזֶה דְּבַר הַשְּׁמִטָּה שָׁמוֹט כָּל־בַּעַל מַשֵּׁה יָדוֹ אֲשֶׁר יַשֶּׁה בְּרֵעֵהוּ
לֹא־יִגֹּשׂ אֶת־רֵעֵהוּ וְאֶת־אָחִיו כִּי־קָרָא שְׁמִטָּה לַיהוָה׃ אֶת־הַנָּכְרִי תִּגֹּשׂ וַאֲשֶׁר יִהְיֶה לְךָ אֶת־אָחִיךָ
תַּשְׁמֵט יָדֶךָ׃ אֶפֶס כִּי לֹא יִהְיֶה־בְּךָ אֶבְיוֹן כִּי־בָרֵךְ יְבָרֶכְךָ יְהוָה בָּאָרֶץ אֲשֶׁר יְהוָה אֱלֹהֶיךָ נֹתֵן־לְךָ נַחֲלָה
לְרִשְׁתָּהּ׃ רַק אִם־שָׁמוֹעַ תִּשְׁמַע בְּקוֹל יְהוָה אֱלֹהֶיךָ לִשְׁמֹר לַעֲשׂוֹת אֶת־כָּל־הַמִּצְוָה הַזֹּאת אֲשֶׁר אָנֹכִי
מְצַוְּךָ הַיּוֹם׃ כִּי־יְהוָה אֱלֹהֶיךָ בֵּרַכְךָ כַּאֲשֶׁר דִּבֶּר־לָךְ וְהַעֲבַטְתָּ גּוֹיִם רַבִּים וְאַתָּה לֹא תַעֲבֹט וּמָשַׁלְתָּ
בְּגוֹיִם רַבִּים וּבְךָ לֹא יִמְשֹׁלוּ׃ כִּי־יִהְיֶה בְךָ אֶבְיוֹן מֵאַחַד אַחֶיךָ בְּאַחַד שְׁעָרֶיךָ בְּאַרְצְךָ אֲשֶׁר־יְהוָה אֱלֹהֶיךָ
נֹתֵן לָךְ לֹא תְאַמֵּץ אֶת־לְבָבְךָ וְלֹא תִקְפֹּץ אֶת־יָדְךָ מֵאָחִיךָ הָאֶבְיוֹן׃ כִּי־פָתֹחַ תִּפְתַּח אֶת־יָדְךָ לוֹ וְהַעֲבֵט
תַּעֲבִיטֶנּוּ דֵּי מַחְסֹרוֹ אֲשֶׁר יֶחְסַר לוֹ׃ הִשָּׁמֶר לְךָ פֶּן־יִהְיֶה דָבָר עִם־לְבָבְךָ בְלִיַּעַל לֵאמֹר קָרְבָה
שְׁנַת־הַשֶּׁבַע שְׁנַת הַשְּׁמִטָּה וְרָעָה עֵינְךָ בְּאָחִיךָ הָאֶבְיוֹן וְלֹא תִתֵּן לוֹ וְקָרָא עָלֶיךָ אֶל־יְהוָה וְהָיָה בְךָ
חֵטְא׃ נָתוֹן תִּתֵּן לוֹ וְלֹא־יֵרַע לְבָבְךָ בְּתִתְּךָ לוֹ כִּי בִּגְלַל | הַדָּבָר הַזֶּה יְבָרֶכְךָ יְהוָה אֱלֹהֶיךָ בְּכָל־מַעֲשֶׂךָ
וּבְכֹל מִשְׁלַח יָדֶךָ׃ כִּי לֹא־יֶחְדַּל אֶבְיוֹן מִקֶּרֶב הָאָרֶץ עַל־כֵּן אָנֹכִי מְצַוְּךָ לֵאמֹר פָּתֹחַ תִּפְתַּח אֶת־יָדְךָ
לְאָחִיךָ לַעֲנִיֶּךָ וּלְאֶבְיֹנְךָ בְּאַרְצֶךָ׃

Every seventh year you shall practice remission of debts. This shall be the nature of the remission: every creditor shall remit the due that he claims from his fellow; he shall not dun his fellow or kinsman, for the remission proclaimed is of the Eternal. You may dun the foreigner; but you must remit whatever is due you from your kinsman. There shall be no needy among you -- since the Eternal your God will bless you in the land that the Eternal your God is giving you as a hereditary portion -- if only you heed the Eternal your God and take care to keep all this Instruction that I enjoin upon you this day. For the Eternal your God will bless you as He has promised you: you will extend loans to many nations, but require none yourself; you will dominate many nations, but they will not dominate you. If, however, there is a needy person among you, one of your kinsmen in any of your settlements in the land that the Eternal your God is giving you, do not harden your heart and shut your hand against your needy kinsman. Rather, you must open your hand and lend him sufficient for whatever he needs. Beware lest you harbor the base thought, "The seventh year, the year of remission, is approaching," so that you are mean to your needy kinsman and give him nothing. He will cry out to the Eternal against you, and you will incur guilt. Give to him readily and have no regrets when you do so, for in return the Eternal your God will bless you in all your efforts and your undertakings. For there will never cease to be needy ones in your land, which is why I command you: open your hand to the poor and needy kinsman in your land.

Deuteronomy 24:19-22

כִּי תִקְצֹר קְצִירְךָ בְשָׂדֶךָ וְשָׁכַחְתָּ עֹמֶר בַּשָּׂדֶה לֹא תָשׁוּב לְקַחְתּוֹ לַגֵּר לַיָּתוֹם וְלָאַלְמָנָה יִהְיֶה לְמַעַן יְבָרֶכְךָ
יְהוָה אֱלֹהֶיךָ בְּכֹל מַעֲשֵׂה יָדֶיךָ׃ כִּי תַחְבֹּט זֵיתְךָ לֹא תְפַאֵר אַחֲרֶיךָ לַגֵּר לַיָּתוֹם וְלָאַלְמָנָה יִהְיֶה׃ כִּי תִבְצֹר
ךָ לֹא תְעוֹלֵל אַחֲרֶיךָ לַגֵּר לַיָּתוֹם וְלָאַלְמָנָה יִהְיֶה׃ וְזָכַרְתָּ כִּי־עֶבֶד הָיִיתָ בְּאֶרֶץ מִצְרָיִם עַל־כֵּן אָנֹכִי
מְצַוְּךָ לַעֲשׂוֹת אֶת־הַדָּבָר הַזֶּה׃ כַּרְמְ

When you reap the harvest in your field and overlook a sheaf in the field, do not turn back to get it; it shall go to the stranger, the fatherless, and the widow -- in order that the Eternal your God may bless you in all your undertakings. When you beat down the fruit of your olive trees, do not go over them again; that shall go to the stranger, the fatherless, and the widow. When you gather the grapes of your vineyard, do not pick it over again; that shall go the stranger, the fatherless, and the widow. Always remember that you were a slave in Egypt; therefore do I enjoin you to observe this commandment.

Appendix II: Transliteration and Glossary

Transliteration:

א = not transliterated
בּ = b
ב = v
ג = g
ד = d
ה = h (also at the end of a word)
ו = v
ז = z
ח = ch
ט = t
י = y
כּ = k
כ = kh
ל = l
מ = m
נ = n
ס = s
ע = not transliterated
פּ = p
פ = f

צ = tz
ק = k
ר = r
שׁ = sh
שׂ = s
תּ or ת = t
ָ = a
short ָ = o
ַ = a
וֹ = o
וּ = u
ֻ = u
ֶ = e
ִ = i
ֵ or ֵי or ֵא = é
ֱ = e
ֳ = o
ֲ = a
vocal sheva = e
silent sheva = not transliterated

In a series of vowels with silent letters, the ' sign is used to aid in pronunciation.

Glossary:

asufi: A foundling.

bét kor: An area large enough to sow thirty *seah* of seed.

chalel: An illegitimate child of a priest.

dinar (pl. *dinarim, dinarin*)*:* A unit of weight and a unit of monetary measurement, a coin.

kav (pl. *kavim*): A basic unit of measurement of volume, equivalent to one-sixtieth of a *seah.*

ketubah: A prenuptial agreement guaranteeing payment by the husband to the wife if he divorces her.

kupah: A coffer for the collection of charity distributed on a weekly basis.

leket: Overlooked gleanings designated for the poor.

litre: A measurement of weight equivalent to one hundred *dinarim.*

log: A basic unit of liquid measurement equivalent to one-fourth of a *kav*.

ma'esar ani: The tithe for the poor. In the third and sixth years of a seven year cycle, after the *terumah* [the priests' share of the produce] and the *ma'asér rishon* [the first tithe given to the Levites] have been taken out, one-tenth of the remainder is designated for the poor.

ma'asér rishon: The first tithe, given to the Levites. After the *terumah* [the priests' share of the produce], has been taken out, one tenth of the remainder is given to the Levites.

ma'asér sheni: The second tithe, taken out after *terumah* [the priests' share of the produce], and *ma'esér rishon* [the first tithe given to the Levites], in the first, second, fourth, and fifth years of a seven year cycle. It was taken by the owner to Jerusalem and eaten there by its owner.

ma'asér tevel: Produce from which the portion due to the priests, *terumah,* was not separated.

mamzer: A child who was conceived in a union forbidden by the Torah.

mitzvah (pl. *mitzvot*): Divine commandment. A positive *mitzvah* is an injunction to do something, and a negative *mitzvah* is a prohibition against doing something.

natin: A descendent of the Gibeonites deemed to have special status under Jewish law.

olélot: Malformed grape clusters designated for the poor.

péah: The edge of a field of grain that is designated for the poor to harvest. It must be something that is edible, raised from the ground, maintained as a crop, gleaned all together at once, and able to be put into storage.

peret: Separated fruit designated for the poor. These are one or two grapes that have become separated or have fallen from a cluster.

seah (pl. *se'in*): A unit of measurement of volume for both dry and liquid measures.

shekel: A unit of measurement of weight and a monetary measurement often equivalent to half of a dinar.

shetuki: An illegitimate child with an unknown father.

shikhecha: Forgotten produce designated for the poor.

tamchui: A plate for the collection of charity distributed on a daily basis.

terumah or *terumah gedolah:* The priests' share of the produce.

terumat ma'asér: The portion the Levites separate from the tithe given to them that they give to the priests.

tzedakah: Charity. The root of this word indicates "righteousness" or "justice."

zuz: A monetary measurement equivalent to a *dinar*.

Appendix III: Editions of Texts and Suggested Reading List

All biblical references are taken from *JPS Hebrew-English Tanakh: The Traditional Hebrew Text and the New JPS Translation* (Philadelphia: the Jewish Publication Society, 1999).

רמב״ם
מדע זרעים
מהדורת ירושלים תשל״דת ד״צ ורשא תרמ״אץ

משנה
על פי ששה סדרי משנה – ע״ג פירושים

תוספתא
זרעים מועדת נשים נזיקין (ב״קת ב״מת ב״ב)

תלמוד בבלי
מסכתות,
ברכות שבת ערובין פסחים יומא סוכה ביצה
ראש השנה תענית מגילה מועד קטן חגיגה
בבא מציעא סנהדרין,
על פי דפוס שטינזל
המבוסס על דפוס וילנא עם מספר שינויים.
פתיחת ראשי תיבותץ
הוספת קטעם שהושמטו על ידי הצנזורהץ
הפסוקים המובאים מהתנ״ךְ נדפסו בכתיב חסרץ
שאר המסכתות,
על פי דפוס וילנאץ

תלמוד ירושלמי
על פי מהדורות וציה רפ״גץ

For further reading:

Cronbach, Abraham. "The Maimonidean Code of Benevolence" in *Hebrew Union College Annual* XX 1947 (New York: Ktav Publishing House, Inc., 1968).

Dorff, Elliot N. *To Do The Right And The Good* (Philadelphia: The Jewish Publication Society, 2001).

Levine, Aaron. *Economics & Jewish Law* (Hoboken: KTAV Publishing House, Inc, 1987, 117-118).

Loewenberg, Frank M. *From Charity To Social Justice: The Emergence of Communal Institutions for the Support of the Poor in Ancient Judaism* (New Brunswick, New Jersey: Transaction Publishers, 2001).

Maimonides, Moses. *The Guide of the Perplexed*, translated by Shlomo Pines (Chicago: The University of Chicago Press, 1963).

Neusner, Jacob. *Tzedakah: Can Jewish Philanthropy Buy Jewish Survival?* (Atlanta: Scholars Press, 1990).

Schechter, Solomon. "Jewish Philanthropy" in *Studies in Judaism*, Third Series (Philadelphia: The Jewish Publication Society of America, 1924).

Sherwin, Byron L. *In Partnership With God* (Syracuse: Syracuse University Press, 1990).

Tamari, Meir. *The Challenge of Wealth: A Jewish Perspective on Earning and Spending Money* (Northvale, New Jersey: Jason Aronson, Inc., 1995).

Twersky, Isadore. *Rabad of Posquiéres: A Twelfth-Century Talmudist* (Cambridge: Harvard University Press, 1962).

Twersky, Isadore. *Studies in Jewish Law and Philosophy* (New York: KTAV Publishing House, Inc., 1982).

Made in the USA
Charleston, SC
28 November 2015